AN EXPOSITION

OF THE

CONSTITUTION OF THE UNITED STATES

Second Edition, Revised.

BY

HENRY FLANDERS,

AUTHOR OF A "TREATISE ON MARITIME LAW," "THE LAW OF SHIPPING," "THE LAW OF FIRE INSURANCE," ETC., ETC.

PHILADELPHIA:
CLAXTON, REMSEN & HAFFELFINGER,
Nos. 624, 626 & 628 MARKET STREET.
1874.

PREFACE.

NO argument would seem to be necessary to prove the importance to the citizens of the United States of an accurate knowledge of the theory and practical character of the Federal Constitution. Either directly or indirectly they participate in the administration of the government which that Constitution has instituted, and surely they should be well grounded in the principles upon which it is founded.

It has been the endeavor of the author in the following pages to supply a convenient manual of instruction to the youth of our country; to make clear and intelligible to the unprofessional reader the fundamental law of our Federative system of government; and at the same time to produce a work which might also be useful to the bar.

In preparing it, he has sought to set forth the reasons upon which each clause of the Constitution rests, as well as the interpretation that has been given to it by the authoritative exposition of the courts, or the well-established practice of the government.

CONTENTS.

CONSTITUTION

OF THE

UNITED STATES OF AMERICA.

We, the people of the United States, in order to form a more perfect Union, establish justice, insure domestic tranquillity, provide for the common defence, promote the general welfare, and secure the blessings of liberty to ourselves and our posterity, do ordain and establish this Constitution for the United States of America.

ARTICLE I.

Section 1.—1. All legislative powers herein granted shall be vested in a Congress of the United States, which shall consist of a Senate and House of Representatives.

Section 2.—1. The House of Representatives shall be composed of members chosen every second year by the people of the several states, and the electors in each state shall have the qualifications requisite for electors of the most numerous branch of the state legislature.

2. No person shall be a Representative who shall not have attained to the age of twenty-five years, and been seven years a citizen of the United States, and who shall not, when elected, be an inhabitant of that state in which he shall be chosen.

3. Representatives and direct taxes shall be apportioned among the several states which may be included within this Union, according to their respective numbers, which shall be determined by adding to the whole number of free persons, including those bound to service for a term of years, and excluding Indians not taxed, three-fifths of all other persons. The actual enumeration shall be made within three years after the first meeting of the Congress of the United States, and within every subsequent term of ten years, in such manner as they shall by law direct. The number of Representatives shall not exceed one for every thirty thousand, but each state shall have at least one Representative; and, until such enumeration shall be made, the state of New Hampshire shall be entitled to choose three, Massachusetts eight, Rhode Island and Providence Plantations one, Connecticut five, New York six, New Jersey four, Pennsylvania eight, Delaware one, Maryland six, Virginia ten, North Carolina five, South Carolina five, and Georgia three.

4. When vacancies happen in the representation from any state, the executive authority thereof shall issue writs of election to fill such vacancies.

5. The House of Representatives shall choose their

Speaker and other officers; and shall have the sole power of impeachment.

SECTION 3.—1. The Senate of the United States shall be composed of two Senators from each state, chosen by the legislature thereof, for six years; and each Senator shall have one vote.

2. Immediately after they shall be assembled in consequence of the first election, they shall be divided, as equally as may be, into three classes. The seats of the Senators of the first class shall be vacated at the expiration of the second year; of the second class, at the expiration of the fourth year; and of the third class, at the expiration of the sixth year; so that one-third may be chosen every second year; and if vacancies happen by resignation, or otherwise, during the recess of the legislature of any state, the executive thereof may make temporary appointments until the next meeting of the legislature, which shall then fill such vacancies.

3. No person shall be a Senator who shall not have attained to the age of thirty years, and been nine years a citizen of the United States, and who shall not, when elected, be an inhabitant of that state for which he shall be chosen.

4. The Vice-President of the United States shall be President of the Senate, but shall have no vote, unless they be equally divided.

5. The Senate shall choose their other officers, and also a President *pro tempore*, in the absence of the Vice-Presi-

dent, or when he shall exercise the office of President of the United States.

6. The Senate shall have the sole power to try all impeachments. When sitting for that purpose, they shall be on oath or affirmation. When the President of the United States is tried, the Chief Justice shall preside; and no person shall be convicted without the concurrence of two-thirds of the members present.

7. Judgment in cases of impeachment shall not extend further than to removal from office, and disqualification to hold and enjoy any office of honor, trust, or profit, under the United States; but the party convicted shall, nevertheless, be liable and subject to indictment, trial, judgment, and punishment, according to law.

SECTION 4.—1. The times, places, and manner, of holding elections for Senators and Representatives, shall be prescribed in each state by the legislature thereof: but the Congress may at any time, by law, make or alter such regulations, except as to the places of choosing Senators.

2. The Congress shall assemble at least once in every year, and such meeting shall be on the first Monday in December, unless they shall by law appoint a different day.

SECTION 5.—1. Each House shall be the judge of the elections, returns, and qualifications of its own members, and a majority of each shall constitute a quorum to do business; but a smaller number may adjourn from day to day, and may be authorized to compel the attendance of absent members, in such manner, and under such penalties, as each House may provide.

2. Each House may determine the rules of its proceedings, punish its members for disorderly behavior, and, with the concurrence of two-thirds, expel a member.

3. Each House shall keep a journal of its proceedings, and, from time to time, publish the same, excepting such parts as may, in their judgment, require secrecy; and the yeas and nays of the members of either House, on any question, shall, at the desire of one-fifth of those present, be entered on the journal.

4. Neither House, during the session of Congress, shall, without the consent of the other, adjourn for more than three days, nor to any other place than that in which the two Houses shall be sitting.

SECTION 6.—1. The Senators and Representatives shall receive a compensation for their services, to be ascertained by law, and paid out of the treasury of the United States. They shall, in all cases, except treason, felony, and breach of the peace, be privileged from arrest during their attendance at the session of their respective Houses, and in going to, and returning from, the same; and for any speech or debate in either House, they shall not be questioned in any other place.

2. No Senator or Representative shall, during the time for which he was elected, be appointed to any civil office under the authority of the United States, which shall have been created, or the emoluments whereof shall have been

increased during such time; and no person, holding any office under the United States, shall be a member of either House during his continuance in office.

SECTION 7.—1. All bills for raising revenue shall originate in the House of Representatives; but the Senate may propose or concur with amendments as on other bills.

2. Every bill, which shall have passed the House of Representatives and the Senate, shall, before it become a law, be presented to the President of the United States; if he approve, he shall sign it, but if not, he shall return it, with his objections, to that House in which it shall have originated, who shall enter the objections at large on their journal, and proceed to reconsider it. If, after such reconsideration, two-thirds of that House shall agree to pass the bill, it shall be sent, together with the objections, to the other House, by which it shall likewise be reconsidered, and, if approved by two-thirds of that House, it shall become a law. But in all such cases the votes of both Houses shall be determined by yeas and nays, and the names of the persons voting for and against the bill shall be entered on the journal of each House respectively. If any bill shall not be returned by the President within ten days (Sundays excepted) after it shall have been presented to him, the same shall be a law, in like manner as if he had signed it, unless the Congress, by their adjournment, prevent its return, in which case it shall not be a law.

3. Every order, resolution, or vote, to which the concurrence of the Senate and House of Representatives may be

necessary (except on a question of adjournment), shall be presented to the President of the United States; and before the same shall take effect, shall be approved by him, or, being disapproved by him, shall be repassed by two-thirds of the Senate and House of Representatives, according to the rules and limitations prescribed in the case of a bill.

SECTION 8.—The Congress shall have power

1. To lay and collect taxes, duties, imposts, and excises, to pay the debts, and provide for the common defence and general welfare, of the United States; but all duties, imposts, and excises, shall be uniform throughout the United States:

2. To borrow money on the credit of the United States:

3. To regulate commerce with foreign nations, and among the several states, and with the Indian tribes:

4. To establish a uniform rule of naturalization, and uniform laws on the subject of bankruptcies, throughout the United States:

5. To coin money, regulate the value thereof, and of foreign coin, and fix the standard of weights and measures:

6. To provide for the punishment of counterfeiting the securities and current coin of the United States:

7. To establish post-offices and post-roads:

8. To promote the progress of science and useful arts, by securing, for limited times, to authors and inventors, the exclusive right to their respective writings and discoveries:

9. To constitute tribunals inferior to the Supreme Court:

10. To define and punish piracies and felonies, committed on the high seas, and offences against the law of nations:

11. To declare war, grant letters of marque and reprisal, and make rules concerning captures on land and water:

12. To raise and support armies; but no appropriation of money to that use shall be for a longer term than two years:

13. To provide and maintain a navy:

14. To make rules for the government and regulation of the land and naval forces:

15. To provide for calling forth the militia to execute the laws of the Union, suppress insurrections, and repel invasions:

16. To provide for organizing, arming, and disciplining the militia, and for governing such part of them as may be employed in the service of the United States, reserving to the states respectively the appointment of the officers, and the authority of training the militia, according to the discipline prescribed by Congress:

17. To exercise exclusive legislation in all cases whatsoever, over such district (not exceeding ten miles square) as may, by cession of particular states, and the acceptance of Congress, become the seat of the government of the United States, and to exercise like authority over all places, purchased by the consent of the legislature of the state in which the same shall be, for the erection of forts, magazines, arsenals, dock-yards, and other needful buildings:—And

18. To make all laws which shall be necessary and proper for carrying into execution the foregoing powers, and all other powers vested by this Constitution in the Government of the United States, or in any department or officer thereof.

SECTION 9.—1. The migration or importation of such persons, as any of the states, now existing, shall think proper to admit, shall not be prohibited by the Congress prior to the year one thousand eight hundred and eight; but a tax or duty may be imposed on such importation, not exceeding ten dollars for each person.

2. The privilege of the writ of *habeas corpus* shall not be suspended, unless when, in cases of rebellion or invasion, the public safety may require it.

3. No bill of attainder, or *ex post facto* law, shall be passed.

4. No capitation, or other direct tax, shall be laid, unless in proportion to the *census* or enumeration hereinbefore directed to be taken.

5. No tax or duty shall be laid on articles exported from any state. No preference shall be given by any regulation of commerce or revenue to the ports of one state over those of another; nor shall vessels bound to, or from, one state, be obliged to enter, clear, or pay duties, in another.

6. No money shall be drawn from the treasury, but in consequence of appropriations made by law; and a regular statement and account of the receipts and expenditures of all public money shall be published from time to time.

7. No title of nobility shall be granted by the United States; and no person, holding any office of profit or trust under them, shall, without the consent of the Congress, accept of any present, emolument, office, or title, of any kind whatever, from any king, prince, or foreign state.

SECTION 10.—1. No state shall enter into any treaty, alliance, or confederation; grant letters of marque and reprisal; coin money; emit bills of credit; make anything but gold and silver coin a tender in payment of debts; pass any bill of attainder, *ex post facto* law, or law impairing the obligation of contracts, or grant any title of nobility.

2. No state shall, without the consent of the Congress, lay any imposts or duties on imports or exports, except what may be absolutely necessary for executing its inspection laws; and the net produce of all duties and imposts, laid by any state on imports or exports, shall be for the use of the treasury of the United States; and all such laws shall be subject to the revision and control of the Congress. No state shall, without the consent of Congress, lay any duty of tonnage, keep troops, or ships of war, in time of peace, enter into any agreement or compact with another state, or with a foreign power, or engage in war, unless actually invaded, or in such imminent danger as will not admit of delay.

ARTICLE II.

SECTION 1.—1. The Executive power shall be vested in a President of the United States of America. He shall hold his office during the term of four years, and together with the Vice-President, chosen for the same term, be elected as follows:

2. Each state shall appoint, in such manner as the legislature thereof may direct, a number of Electors, equal to the whole number of Senators and Representatives, to which the state may be entitled in the Congress; but no Senator or Representative, or person holding an office of trust or profit, under the United States, shall be appointed an Elector.

3. The Electors shall meet in their respective states, and vote by ballot for two persons, of whom one, at least, shall not be an inhabitant of the same state with themselves. And they shall make a list of all the persons voted for, and of the number of votes for each; which list they shall sign and certify, and transmit, sealed, to the seat of the Government of the United States, directed to the President of the Senate. The President of the Senate shall, in the presence of the Senate and House of Representatives, open all the certificates, and the votes shall then be counted. The person having the greatest number of votes shall be the President, if such number be a majority of the whole number of Electors appointed; and if there be more than one, who have such majority, and have an equal number of votes, then the House of Representatives shall immediately choose, by ballot, one of them for President; and if no person have a majority, then, from the five highest on the list, the said House shall, in like manner, choose the President. But in choosing the President, the votes shall be taken by states, the representation from each state having one vote; a quorum for this

purpose shall consist of a member or members from two-thirds of the states, and a majority of all the states shall be necessary to a choice. In every case, after the choice of the President, the person having the greatest number of votes of the Electors shall be the Vice-President. But if there should remain two or more who have equal votes, the Senate shall choose from them, by ballot, the Vice-President.

4. The Congress may determine the time of choosing the Electors, and the day on which they shall give their votes; which day shall be the same throughout the United States.

5. No person, except a natural-born citizen, or a citizen of the United States at the time of the adoption of this Constitution, shall be eligible to the office of President; neither shall any person be eligible to that office, who shall not have attained to the age of thirty-five years, and been fourteen years a resident within the United States.

6. In case of the removal of the President from office, or of his death, resignation, or inability to discharge the powers and duties of the said office, the same shall devolve on the Vice-President, and the Congress may by law provide for the case of removal, death, resignation, or inability, both of the President and Vice-President, declaring what officer shall then act as President, and such officer shall act accordingly, until the disability be removed, or a President shall be elected.

7. The President shall, at stated times, receive for his services, a compensation, which shall neither be increased nor diminished during the period for which he shall have

been elected, and he shall not receive, within that period, any other emolument from the United States, or any of them.

8. Before he enter on the execution of his office, he shall take the following oath or affirmation:

9. "I do solemnly swear (or affirm), that I will faithfully execute the office of President of the United States, and will, to the best of my ability, preserve, protect, and defend the Constitution of the United States."

SECTION 2.—1. The President shall be Commander-in-Chief of the army and navy of the United States, and of the militia of the several states, when called into the actual service of the United States; he may require the opinion, in writing, of the principal officer in each of the executive departments upon any subject relating to the duties of their respective offices, and he shall have power to grant reprieves and pardons for offences against the United States, except in cases of impeachment.

2. He shall have power, by and with the advice and consent of the Senate, to make treaties, provided two-thirds of the Senators present concur; and he shall nominate, and, by and with the advice and consent of the Senate, shall appoint ambassadors, other public ministers, and consuls, judges of the Supreme Court, and all other officers of the United States whose appointments are not herein otherwise provided for, and which shall be established by law: but the Congress may by law vest the appointment of such inferior officers, as they think proper, in the President alone, in the courts of law, or in the heads of departments.

3. The President shall have power to fill up all vacancies that may happen during the recess of the Senate, by granting commissions which shall expire at the end of their next session.

SECTION 3.—1. He shall, from time to time, give to the Congress information of the state of the Union, and recommend to their consideration such measures as he shall judge necessary and expedient; he may, on extraordinary occasions, convene both Houses, or either of them, and in case of disagreement between them, with respect to the time of adjournment, he may adjourn them to such time as he shall think proper; he shall receive ambassadors and other public ministers; he shall take care that the laws be faithfully executed, and shall commission all the officers of the United States.

SECTION 4.—1. The President, Vice-President, and all civil officers of the United States, shall be removed from office on impeachment for, and conviction of, treason, bribery, or other high crimes and misdemeanors.

ARTICLE III.

SECTION 1.—1. The judicial power of the United States shall be vested in one Supreme Court, and in such inferior courts as the Congress may, from time to time, ordain and establish. The judges, both of the Supreme and inferior courts, shall hold their offices during good behavior, and shall, at stated times, receive for their services a compensation which shall not be diminished during their continuance in office.

SECTION 2.—1. The judicial power shall extend to all cases, in law and equity, arising under this Constitution, the laws of the United States, and treaties made, or which shall be made, under their authority; to all cases affecting ambassadors, other public ministers, and consuls; to all cases of admiralty and maritime jurisdiction; to controversies to which the United States shall be a party; to controversies between two or more states, between a state and citizens of another state, between citizens of different states, between citizens of the same state claiming lands under grants of different states, and between a state, or the citizens thereof, and foreign states, citizens, or subjects.

2. In all cases affecting ambassadors, other public ministers and consuls, and those in which a state shall be a party, the Supreme Court shall have original jurisdiction. In all the other cases before mentioned, the Supreme Court shall have appellate jurisdiction, both as to law and fact, with such exceptions and under such regulations as the Congress shall make.

3. The trial of all crimes, except in cases of impeachment, shall be by jury; and such trial shall be held in the state where the said crimes shall have been committed; but when not committed within any state the trial shall be at such place or places as the Congress may by law have directed.

SECTION 3.—1. Treason against the United States shall consist only in levying war against them, or in adhering to their enemies, giving them aid and comfort. No person shall be convicted of treason unless on the testimony of two witnesses to the same overt act, or on confession in open court.

2. The Congress shall have power to declare the punishment of treason, but no attainder of treason shall work corruption of blood or forfeiture, except during the life of the person attainted.

ARTICLE IV.

SECTION 1.—1. Full faith and credit shall be given in each state to the public acts, records, and judicial proceedings of every other state. And the Congress may, by general laws, prescribe the manner in which such acts, records, and proceedings shall be proved, and the effect thereof.

SECTION 2.—1. The citizens of each state shall be entitled to all privileges and immunities of citizens in the several states.

2. A person charged in any state with treason, felony, or other crime, who shall flee from justice, and be found in another state, shall, on demand of the executive authority of the state from which he fled, be delivered up, to be removed to the state having jurisdiction of the crime.

3. No person held to service or labor in one state, under the laws thereof, escaping into another, shall, in consequence of any law or regulation therein, be discharged from such service or labor, but shall be delivered up on claim of the party to whom such service or labor may be due.

SECTION 3.—1. New states may be admitted by the Congress into this Union; but no new state shall be formed or erected within the jurisdiction of any other state; nor any state be formed by the junction of two or more states, or parts of states, without the consent of the legislatures of the states concerned as well as of the Congress.

2. The Congress shall have power to dispose of and make all needful rules and regulations respecting the territory or other property belonging to the United States; and nothing in this Constitution shall be so construed as to prejudice any claims of the United States, or of any particular state.

SECTION 4.—1. The United States shall guarantee to every state in this Union a republican form of government, and shall protect each of them against invasion; and on application of the legislature, or of the executive (when the legislature cannot be convened), against domestic violence.

ARTICLE V.

1. The Congress, whenever two-thirds of both Houses shall deem it necessary, shall propose amendments to this Constitution, or, on the application of the legislatures of two-thirds of the several states, shall call a convention for proposing amendments, which, in either case, shall be valid, to all intents and purposes, as part of this Constitution, when ratified by the legislatures of three-fourths of the several states, or by conventions in three-fourths thereof, as the one or the other mode of ratification may be proposed by the Congress: provided that no amendment which may be made prior to the year one thousand eight hundred and eight, shall, in any manner, affect the first and fourth

clauses in the ninth section of the first Article; and that no state, without its consent, shall be deprived of its equal suffrage in the Senate.

ARTICLE VI.

1. All debts contracted and engagements entered into, before the adoption of this Constitution, shall be as valid against the United States under this Constitution as under the Confederation.

2. This Constitution, and the laws of the United States which shall be made in pursuance thereof, and all treaties made, or which shall be made, under the authority of the United States, shall be the supreme law of the land; and the judges in every state shall be bound thereby, anything in the constitution or laws of any state to the contrary notwithstanding.

3. The Senators and Representatives before mentioned, and the members of the several state legislatures, and all executive and judicial officers, both of the United States and of the several states, shall be bound, by oath or affirmation, to support this Constitution; but no religious test shall ever be required as a qualification to any office or public trust under the United States.

ARTICLE VII.

1. The ratification of the conventions of nine states shall be sufficient for the establishment of this Constitution between the states so ratifying the same.

AMENDMENTS TO THE CONSTITUTION.

ARTICLE I.

Congress shall make no law respecting an establishment of religion, or prohibiting the free exercise thereof; or abridging the freedom of speech, or of the press; or the right of the people peaceably to assemble, and to petition the government for a redress of grievances.

ARTICLE II.

A well-regulated militia being necessary to the security of a free state, the right of the people to keep and bear arms shall not be infringed.

ARTICLE III.

No soldier shall, in time of peace, be quartered in any house, without the consent of the owner; nor, in time of war, but in a manner to be prescribed by law.

ARTICLE IV.

The right of the people to be secure in their persons, houses, papers, and effects, against unreasonable searches and seizures, shall not be violated; and no warrants shall issue, but upon probable cause, supported by oath or affirmation, and particularly describing the place to be searched, and the persons or things to be seized.

ARTICLE V.

No person shall be held to answer for a capital, or otherwise infamous, crime, unless on a presentment or indictment of a grand jury, except in cases arising in the land or naval forces, or in the militia, when in actual service, in time of war, or public danger; nor shall any person be subject, for the same offence, to be twice put in jeopardy of life or limb; nor shall be compelled, in any criminal case, to be a witness against himself, nor be deprived of life, liberty, or property, without due process of law; nor shall private property be taken for public use, without just compensation.

ARTICLE VI.

In all criminal prosecutions, the accused shall enjoy the right to a speedy and public trial, by an impartial jury of the state and district wherein the crime shall have been committed, which district shall have been previously ascertained by law; and to be informed of the nature and cause of the accusation; to be confronted with the witnesses against him; to have compulsory process for obtaining witnesses in his favor; and to have the assistance of counsel for his defence.

ARTICLE VII.

In suits at common law, where the value in controversy

shall exceed twenty dollars, the right of trial by jury shall be preserved; and no fact, tried by a jury, shall be otherwise re-examined in any court of the United States than according to the rules of the common law.

ARTICLE VIII.

Excessive bail shall not be required, nor excessive fines imposed, nor cruel and unusual punishments inflicted.

ARTICLE IX.

The enumeration in the Constitution of certain rights shall not be construed to deny or disparage others retained by the people.

ARTICLE X.

The powers not delegated to the United States by the Constitution, nor prohibited by it to the states, are reserved to the states respectively, or to the people.

ARTICLE XI.

The judicial power of the United States shall not be construed to extend to any suit in law or equity, commenced or prosecuted against one of the United States by citizens of another state, or by citizens or subjects of any foreign state.

ARTICLE XII.

1. The Electors shall meet in their respective states, and vote by ballot for President and Vice-President, one of whom, at least, shall not be an inhabitant of the same state with themselves; they shall name in their ballots the person

voted for as President, and in distinct ballots the person voted for as Vice-President; and they shall make distinct lists of all persons voted for as President, and of all persons voted for as Vice-President, and of the number of votes for each, which lists they shall sign, and certify, and transmit, sealed, to the seat of the Government of the United States, directed to the President of the Senate; the President of the Senate shall, in the presence of the Senate and House of Representatives, open all the certificates, and the votes shall then be counted; the person having the greatest number of votes for President shall be the President, if such number be a majority of the whole number of Electors appointed; and if no person have such a majority, then, from the persons having the highest numbers, not exceeding three, on the list of those voted for as President, the House of Representatives shall choose immediately, by ballot, the President. But in choosing the President, the votes shall be taken by states, the representation from each state having one vote; a quorum for this purpose shall consist of a member or members from two-thirds of the states, and a majority of all the states shall be necessary to a choice. And if the House of Representatives shall not choose a President, whenever the right of choice shall devolve upon them, before the fourth day of March next following, then the Vice-President shall act as President, as in case of the death, or other constitutional disability, of the President.

2 The person having the greatest number of votes as

Vice-President shall be the Vice-President, if such number be a majority of the whole number of Electors appointed; and if no person have a majority, then, from the two highest numbers on the list, the Senate shall choose the Vice-President; a quorum for the purpose shall consist of two-thirds of the whole number of Senators; a majority of the whole number shall be necessary to a choice.

3. But no person constitutionally ineligible to the office of President, shall be eligible to that of Vice-President of the United States.

ARTICLE XIII.

SECTION 1.—Neither slavery nor involuntary servitude, except as a punishment for crime, whereof the party shall have been duly convicted, shall exist within the United States, or any place subject to their jurisdiction.

SECTION 2.—Congress shall have power to enforce this article by appropriate legislation.

ARTICLE XIV.

SECTION 1.—All persons born or naturalized in the United States, and subject to the jurisdiction thereof, are citizens of the United States and of the state wherein they reside. No state shall make or enforce any law which shall abridge the privileges or immunities of citizens of the United States; nor shall any state deprive any person of life, liberty, or property, without due process of law, nor deny to any person within its jurisdiction the equal protection of the laws.

SECTION 2.—Representatives shall be apportioned among the several states according to their respective numbers, counting the whole number of persons in each state, excluding Indians not taxed. But when the right to vote at any election for the choice of electors for President and Vice-President of the United States, Representatives in Congress, the executive and judicial officers of a state, or the members of the legislature thereof, is denied to any of the male inhabitants of such state, being twenty-one years of age, and citizens of the United States, or in any way abridged, except for participation in rebellion or other crime, the basis of representation therein shall be reduced in the proportion which the number of such male citizens shall bear to the whole number of male citizens twenty-one years of age in such state.

SECTION 3.—No person shall be a Senator or Representative in Congress, or elector of President and Vice-President, or hold any office, civil or military, under the United States, or under any state, who, having previously taken an oath, as a member of Congress, or as an officer of the United States, or as a member of any state legislature, or as an executive or judicial officer of any state, to support the Constitution of the United States, shall have engaged in insurrection or rebellion against the same, or given aid or comfort to the enemies thereof. But Congress may, by a vote of two-thirds of each House, remove such disability.

SECTION 4.—The validity of the public debt of the United States, authorized by law, including debts incurred for payment of pensions and bounties for services in suppressing insurrection or rebellion, shall not be questioned. But neither the United States nor any state shall assume or pay any debt or obligation incurred in aid of insurrection or rebellion against the United States, or any claim for the loss or emancipation of any slave; but all such debts, obligations, and claims shall be held illegal and void.

SECTION 5.—The Congress shall have power to enforce, by appropriate legislation, the provisions of this article.

ARTICLE XV.

SECTION 1.—The right of citizens of the United States to vote shall not be denied or abridged by the United States or by any state on account of race, color, or previous condition of servitude.

SECTION 2.—The Congress shall have power to enforce this article by appropriate legislation.

AN

EXPOSITION OF THE CONSTITUTION.

ITS ORIGIN.

The Union of the Colonies.

1. THE impolitic course of Great Britain towards her North American colonies led to that correspondence, and, finally, to that union between them, which has proved, in large measure, the source of their power and prosperity. Accustomed, however, anterior to the Revolution, to a separate, independent existence, each colony having its distinct government, they still maintained that separate political existence, notwithstanding they united their counsels and resources for the common defence and general welfare.

The Stamp-act Congress.

2. The attempt of England to derive a revenue from the colonies by means of a tax on stamps, led a

majority, namely, nine of the colonial assemblies, to send delegates to a Congress which assembled at New York, in October, 1765, to consult together, and make a common representation to implore relief. The determined attitude of the colonies on this occasion, and their resolute denial and resistance to the assumed right of taxation, induced Parliament to repeal the obnoxious act.

3. But little more than a year elapsed, however, before the project of taxation was again revived, and early in the year 1767 Parliament passed another act, with the avowed object of deriving a revenue from America. This measure re-opened the fountain of discontent and controversy, and led to that resistance on the one hand, and those attempts at coercion on the other, which at last resulted in open war, and the dismemberment of the British Empire.

The Continental Congress.

4. On the 5th of September, 1774, delegates from all the colonies, except Georgia, assembled at Philadelphia to deliberate upon the state of public affairs, and devise and recommend measures of relief. The method of voting in this Congress was by colonies, that is, each colony had one vote. In pursuance of their authority, they adopted resolutions defining their rights and the foundation of them. They de-

clared the several instances in which those rights had been violated. For the redress of their wrongs they entered into a non-importation, non-consumption, and non-exportation agreement. They prepared an address to the people of Great Britain, a memorial to the inhabitants of British America, and a petition to the king.

5. If these measures should prove unsuccessful, and their grievances remain unredressed, they recommended that another Congress should be held on the 10th of the following May. The British government still persisting in their system, a second Congress, composed of delegates from twelve colonies, accordingly assembled at Philadelphia in May, 1775. In the course of the year Georgia united with her sister colonies, and sent delegates to the Congress.

Powers exercised by the Congress.

6. The second Continental Congress exercised for nearly six years, that is, from their meeting until the final ratification of the Articles of Confederation on the 1st of March, 1781, the powers of a supreme, controlling national council. They declared the colonies free and independent states, raised armies, made treaties, and performed the highest acts of sovereign authority. They did all this, without any express delegation of power, but with the implied

sanction of their constituents, who acquiesced in, and approved their proceedings.

The Articles of Confederation.

7. The powers of Congress remained undefined until the adoption of the Articles of Confederation, which then became the rule of government. These Articles were laid before Congress by a committee of their body on the 12th of July, 1776; and after being debated and amended from time to time, they were finally agreed to on the 17th of November, 1777, and submitted to the legislatures of the states for their ratification.

8. The state legislatures, at successive dates, authorized their delegates in Congress to ratify them; but the ratifications were not completed until the 1st of March, 1781. Congress assembled under their authority on the following day; but it was soon discovered that the powers which they now possessed were totally inadequate to the purposes of an efficient government.

Powers confided to the Confederation.

9. Each state retained every power, right, and jurisdiction not expressly delegated to Congress. And the powers actually delegated were restricted in their exercise. Thus Congress could never engage

in war, nor grant letters of marque and reprisal in time of peace, nor enter into any treaties or alliances, nor coin money, nor regulate the value thereof, nor ascertain the sums and expenses necessary for the defence and welfare of the United States or any of them, nor emit bills, nor borrow money on the credit of the United States, nor appropriate money, nor agree upon the number of vessels of war to be built or purchased, or the number of land or sea forces to be raised, nor appoint a commander-in-chief of the army or navy, without the assent of nine states, each state having one vote.

10. But even after the assent of the requisite number of states, Congress, having no coercive authority, could not execute its most important measures. The concurrence of thirteen distinct sovereignties was necessary in order to give them effect.

11. Congress, for example, could declare war, but it depended upon the states whether they should have an army and navy; they could make treaties, but it equally depended upon the states whether they should be observed; they could contract debts, and again it depended upon the states whether they should be paid.

12. They could lay and collect no taxes, the states reserving this power to themselves. They

could only ascertain the sums necessary to be raised for the service of the United States, and call on the several states for their respective proportions thereof. Whether the several states would respond to this call at all, or at what time, or in what manner, depended wholly upon themselves.

13. Another great defect in the Articles of Confederation was the want of any power in Congress to regulate foreign and domestic commerce. This led to conflicting and irritating regulations on the part of the several states, and threatened the most serious consequences.

Result of the Confederation.

14. In short, the government of the Confederation possessed in reality only a power of recommendation, and hence the efficacy of its measures depended upon their being in harmony with the views, interests, and convenience of the several states.

15. The result was natural: the measures of the Congress were not executed. That body was unsupplied with the means to pay the public debt, and possessed neither respect abroad, nor credit and confidence at home. "In a word," said Washington, "the Confederation appears to me to be little more than a shadow without the substance; and Congress a nugatory body, their ordinances being little attended to."

Origin of the Convention which framed the Constitution.

16. In this emergency, a Convention which had assembled at Annapolis in the autumn of 1786, to devise a uniform system of commercial regulations, in consequence of imperfect powers, and an inadequate representation, forbore to consider that subject, but instead thereof recommended the appointment of commissioners from all the states, to devise such additional provisions as should appear to them necessary to render the Constitution of the Federal Government adequate to the exigencies of the Union.

17. This action of the Annapolis Convention met with a favorable response. On the 21st of the following February, Congress formally recommended a convention of delegates, to be appointed by the several states, for the sole and express purpose of revising the Articles of Confederation, and reporting to Congress and the several legislatures such alterations and provisions therein, as should, when agreed to in Congress and confirmed by the states under the Federal Constitution, seem adequate to the exigencies of the government and the preservation of the Union.

The Meeting and Result of the Convention.

18. Delegates were accordingly appointed by the several state legislatures, except the legislature of Rhode Island, who assembled in convention at Philadelphia, in May, 1787. This Convention, which was composed of the most distinguished abilities of the country, continued in session nearly four months.

19. The Constitution, or plan of government, which they framed, was finally adopted on the 17th of September, 1787. It was then laid before the Congress of the Confederation, together with the opinion of the Convention that it should be submitted to a convention of delegates, chosen in each state by the people thereof, under the recommendation of its legislature, for their assent and ratification. This mode of proceeding was adopted, and the Constitution was thus submitted to the people of the several states. They acted upon it, through delegates assembled in convention within their respective states. From these conventions the Constitution derives its whole authority. By their assent and ratification it became of complete obligation, and bound the state sovereignties.

Organization of the Government.

20. Eleven of the states, that is, all but North Carolina and Rhode Island, having notified Congress of their ratification of the Constitution, that body, on the 13th of September, 1788, passed a resolution appointing the first Wednesday in January following, for the choice of Electors of President; the first Wednesday in February following, for the assembling of the Electors to vote for a President; and the first Wednesday in March following, for the government, under the Constitution, to go into operation.

21. Electors were accordingly chosen in the several states, who met at the designated time and voted for President and Vice-President. George Washington, as afterwards appeared upon opening and counting the votes, was unanimously elected President, and John Adams was elected Vice-President. Senators and Representatives were also duly chosen in the several states, and the First Congress assembled at New York, then the seat of government, on the 4th of March, 1789, when the Constitution went into legal operation.

22. A quorum of the House of Representatives, however, was not formed until the first of April, nor of the Senate until the 6th. Several months, too, elapsed before Congress could pass the necessary

laws for organizing the judiciary and the several executive departments. But, in the course of a year, the machinery, so to speak, of the new government was adjusted and put in harmonious operation. In November, 1789, North Carolina, through her convention, ratified the Constitution, and Rhode Island followed her example in May, 1790. And thus the original circle of thirteen states was completed.

THE OBJECT FOR WHICH THE CONSTITUTION WAS ORDAINED.

Definitions.

23. Government may be briefly defined as the power or authority which rules a community. When there is no control upon the persons who exercise this power or authority but their own will, the government is arbitrary. On the contrary, when the methods and the limits, within which they must exercise it, are marked out and prescribed, the government is constitutional, no matter what particular form it may assume.

24. A constitution, then, may be defined as the rule which limits the action and prescribes the powers and duties of a government, and the methods by which those powers and duties shall be administered.

How Constitutions originate.

25. It is not necessary that a constitution should be written or exist in visible form. On the contrary, the instances are rare, in the history of mankind, of a constitution being drawn up in a formal manner, and for the purpose of instituting a new form of

government. For the most part constitutions have grown out of successive modifications of pre-existing governments.

26. An arbitrary government, for example, becoming intolerable, the community rise and demand some security against its oppressions. They insist upon a curtailment of its powers, and some provision for their protection. Such curtailment and provision amount, in fact, to a constitution, however imperfect it may be. As time develops its defects further changes take place, until, at length, it becomes, in greater or less measure, adapted to the wants and situation of the particular community.

27. The Roman constitution came into being in this manner, and though never existing in visible form, yet the respective powers of the senate, consuls, tribunes, and assemblies of the people were as well defined perhaps by usage and particular decrees as if they had been written upon parchment or engraven upon stone. The English constitution, too, is the growth of centuries, and is the combined product of custom, tradition, judicial decisions, royal grants, and legislative acts.

28. The Constitution of the United States, on the other hand, instituted the government itself, and may be termed a Constitution of written Articles, which set forth the principles upon which the

government shall be organized and administered, and the powers and duties of its respective departments.

For what Purpose the Constitution was established.

29. It was ordained and established by the people of the United States, in order to form a more perfect Union, establish justice, insure domestic tranquillity, provide for the common defence, promote the general welfare, and secure the blessings of liberty to themselves and their posterity.

30. Such being the purpose, what means have been devised to attain it? In the first place, the powers with which the government is invested are divided among distinct and separate departments, each acting as a control on the others. These departments are legislative, executive, and judicial. We shall consider them in the order they are presented in the Constitution itself.

31. It is proper to observe, however, in this place, that when the Constitution declares the purpose for which it was ordained and established, such declaration neither confers nor enlarges any power confided to any department of the government, but is merely explanatory of the objects for which those powers were conferred, and thus constitutes an important key to their interpretation.

THE LEGISLATURE.

Distribution of Legislative Power.

32. All legislative powers granted by the Constitution are vested in a Congress of the United States, which consists of a Senate and House of Representatives.

Importance of two Branches.

33. Several eminent characters have deemed a division of legislative power between two branches, each having a negative on the other, as unwise and unnecessary. A legislature with two branches, said Dr. Franklin, is a wagon drawn by a horse before and a horse behind, in opposite directions. But reason and experience have alike demonstrated the correctness of the contrary opinion.

34. It is now generally conceded that a division of legislative power is essential in order to prevent those errors and mistakes which a single assembly is liable to commit from haste or inattention, or those impolitic and dangerous acts of legislation into which it may be hurried by the impulses of feeling, by surprise, by intrigue, by fervid eloquence within doors, or the pressure of opinion without.

35. With two branches, it is obvious that each will act with more caution and deliberation, in order that its measures may justify the approval of the other. To make this mutual check and control more effectual, the two branches ought to be instituted upon different principles, so that the same influences which operate upon the one shall be less potential with the other.

36. The framers of the Constitution of the United States were not inattentive to this consideration when they made the term of office, the qualifications, and mode of election for a senator different from what are prescribed for a representative. We shall presently see that in all these particulars the two houses of Congress are constituted differently.

THE HOUSE OF REPRESENTATIVES.

When and by whom Chosen.

37. The House of Representatives is composed of members chosen every second year by the people of the several states, and the electors in each state must have the qualifications requisite for electors of the most numerous branch of the state legislature.

Dependence of the Representative upon the Constituent.

38. Without a dependence of the representative upon the electors, without a power on their part to call him to account for his conduct, the experiment of republican government would be likely to end in an oligarchy or a despotism. A permanent legislative body, though they may, like the Council of Venice, advance the power of a country, are a most unsafe custodian of its liberties.

39. Hence it has become an axiom in republican states that the representative should be directly responsible to the people, and this responsibility is ensured by the frequency of his election.

How frequently should a Representative be elected?

40. How frequent this election should be, or how long should be the duration of a representative's term of office, is a question that does not admit of an exact solution. It may be affirmed, however, as a general proposition, that it should never be so long as to destroy his sense of dependence on his constituents, nor so short as to prevent that familiarity with the practical business of legislation, and that knowledge of the interests of his country upon which his usefulness must essentially depend.

41. The framers of the Constitution, in establishing biennial elections for representatives, were influenced, in part, by the known attachment of the people to the principle of frequent elections. Most of the states chose their representatives annually, Connecticut and Rhode Island semi-annually, North and South Carolina biennially, and Virginia alone septennially.

42. It would, therefore, have been impolitic, and have heightened the opposition which the Constitution encountered when submitted to the people for their assent and ratification, if the term of service in the House of Representatives had been fixed at a longer period than two years. Besides, in fixing

upon that term, it was thought that the inconvenience of a too frequent election on the one hand, and a too long duration of power on the other, would be, in great measure, guarded against.

Qualifications for Electors.

43. It will be remarked that the electors of representatives in each state must possess the same qualifications as the electors of the most numerous branch of the state legislature. Originally the qualifications for electors were different in the different states; and if the Constitution had disregarded these differences and established a uniform qualification for all, it would have been likely to cause great dissatisfaction. But, the states themselves have since made great changes in the qualifications of their electors, and they now approach to a nearly uniform standard: universal suffrage prevailing in all or most of the states. Moreover, by the fifteenth amendment, which was declared duly ratified by the requisite number of States on the 30th day of March, 1870, it is declared that the right of citizens of the United States to vote shall not be denied or abridged by the United States, or by any State, on account of race, color, or previous condition of servitude. So that by the terms in effect of this amendment any restriction upon the elective franchise on these grounds is forbidden.

Qualifications for a Representative.

44. No person can be a Representative who has not attained the age of twenty-five years, and been seven years a citizen of the United States. He must also, when elected, be an inhabitant of the state in which he is chosen.

45. Three qualifications are thus required on the part of a representative:

First, He must have attained the age of twenty-five.

Secondly, He must have been seven years a citizen of the United States. A foreigner is thus eligible to the House of Representatives after a citizenship of seven years; but he is not a citizen until he has been naturalized, and to be naturalized requires a previous residence of five years. So that twelve years must elapse before he is eligible as a Representative.

46. Thirdly, He must, when elected, be an inhabitant of the state in which he shall be chosen; that is, he must really be a member of the state, subject to all the requisitions of its laws, and entitled to all the privileges and advantages which they confer. By a political fiction, however, a representative of his country at a foreign court, though residing abroad, is still regarded, as it were, as being at home. He remains under the jurisdiction and laws of his own

country, like a sailor upon the high seas, and is not subject to the laws of the country in which he resides. Hence he is not deemed, by his foreign residence, to lose his character of inhabitant of the state of which he is a citizen, and may be elected to a seat in Congress. In addition to the qualifications thus specified, the fourteenth amendment, which was declared a part of the Constitution on the 28th day of July, 1868, provides that no person shall be a Senator or Representative in Congress, or elector of President and Vice-President, or hold any office, civil or military, under the United States, or under any state, who, having previously taken an oath, as a member of Congress, or as an officer of the United States, or as a member of any state legislature, or as an executive or judicial officer of any state, to support the Constitution of the United States, shall have engaged in insurrection or rebellion against the same, or given aid or comfort to the enemies thereof. The disability, however, created by this amendment Congress may remove by a vote of two-thirds of each house.*

47. The Constitution having fixed the qualifications for a Representative, the states cannot require others. They can neither add to, nor in any manner vary the qualifications set forth in the Constitution itself. They cannot, for example, require their

---

* Ohio and New Jersey withdrew their consent to this amendment before its proclamation.

representatives to be freeholders or professors of any particular religious belief, or inhabitants of the particular districts from which they are chosen, in addition to being inhabitants of the state, because in this instance the affirmation of certain qualifications obviously implies a negation of all others.

Apportionment of Representatives.

48. The apportionment of representatives among the several states was a subject of great difficulty. It was generally agreed that the apportionment should be made according to their respective numbers; but how should these numbers be determined? On the one hand it was contended that slaves were property, and as representation was to be based on persons, they ought to be excluded from the enumeration equally with all other property.

49. On the other hand it was urged that in the union of independent states, the population of each should constitute the basis of its representation in the common legislature, without reference to its condition. Slaves, it was said, were the laboring, producing population of many of the states, and constituted a large portion of their aggregate numbers. Hence, it was contended, that it would be unjust to these states to exclude the slaves from the census.

Slaves regarded in the Apportionment.

50. After an exciting controversy the subject was compromised as follows: The slaveholding states were allowed a representation for three-fifths of their slaves; but it was agreed at the same time that they should pay direct taxes in the same proportion. Thus the increase in the number of their representatives was accompanied by a corresponding increase in the amount of their direct taxes.

51. That is, representatives and direct taxes are apportioned among the several states, according to their respective numbers, which are determined by adding to the whole number of free persons, including those bound to service for a term of years, and excluding Indians not taxed, three-fifths of all other persons, meaning thereby slaves. As, however, slavery was abolished by the thirteenth amendment, which was declared a part of the Constitution of the United States on the 18th day of December, A. D. 1865, it became necessary to apportion representatives among the several states upon a basis different from that provided in the original Constitution. Accordingly, by the terms of the fourteenth amendment, it is declared as follows: Representatives shall be apportioned among the several states according to their respective numbers, counting the whole number of persons in each state, excluding Indians not taxed. But when

the right to vote at any election for the choice of electors for President and Vice-President of the United States, Representatives in Congress, the executive and judicial officers of a state, or the members of the legislature thereof, is denied to any of the male inhabitants of such state, being twenty-one years of age, and citizens of the United States, or in any way abridged, except for participation in rebellion or other crime, the basis of representation therein shall be reduced in the proportion which the number of such male citizens shall bear to the whole number of male citizens twenty-one years of age in such state.

Limit as to number of Representatives.

52. The number of representatives is not to exceed one for every thirty thousand; but each state is entitled to at least one.

A Census required to be taken.

53. To ascertain the population of the respective states, and apportion representatives among them according to their relative increase of numbers, an enumeration is required to be made, every ten years, in such manner as Congress shall by law direct.

54. The first enumeration was made in 1790, and has since been made once in every ten years, as the Constitution requires.

Mode of Apportionment.

55. Though, at first view, it would seem to be a very easy matter to apportion representatives among the states, according to their respective numbers, it has nevertheless been a subject of much difficulty. In point of fact, it has been found impracticable to apportion representatives exactly according to numbers. Whatever common ratio or divisor is fixed upon, there will be resulting fractions. If these fractions are less than thirty thousand they must be disregarded, because, by the Constitution, more representatives than one for every thirty thousand are not allowed. But if the fractions exceed thirty thousand what is to be done with them?

56. The rule adopted by Congress, at one time, was this: the representative population of each state was divided by a common divisor, and, in addition to the number of members resulting from such division, a member was allowed to each state whose fraction exceeded a moiety of the division.

57. By the present law (Feb. 2, 1872,) it is provided that after the 3d day of March, 1873, the House of Representatives shall be composed of two hundred and eighty-three members. These members are apportioned among the several states according to the ninth census, and the number each state is entitled to is specifically stated in the act. If a new state is ad-

mitted into the Union subsequent to such apportionment, the representation or representatives of such new state are additional to the original number of two hundred and eighty-three.*

58. In addition to the representation of the states, Congress allow each of the organized territories of the United States to send a delegate to the House of Representatives, who has the privilege of debating but not of voting.

Vacancies.

59. To conclude this branch of our subject we have only to add, that when vacancies happen in the representation from any state, the executive authority thereof is required to issue writs of election to

* By the act of May 23, 1850, the number of representatives of which the House was to be composed was fixed at 233. The aggregate representative population of the United States, ascertained by adding to the whole number of free persons in all the states, including those bound to service for a term of years, and excluding Indians not taxed, three-fifths of all other persons, was divided by 233, and the quotient, rejecting fractions, became the ratio of representatives among the several states. The representative population of each state, ascertained in the same manner, being now divided by this common ratio, gave the number of representatives apportioned to each. But in this process there had been a loss in the number of members caused by the fractions; it fell short of 233. This loss was compensated for by assigning to so many states having the largest fractions as might be necessary to make the whole number of representatives 233, one additional member each for its fraction

fill them; and also, that the house of representatives choose their own speaker and other officers, and have the sole power of impeachment. It may also be observed, that it is not necessary for the executive of a state to be first informed by the house itself that a vacancy exists before issuing a writ of election; it is sufficient if he has received the resignation of a member.

THE SENATE.

Importance of a Senate.

60. Mr. Burke has remarked that a monarchy may exist without a senate; but that it seems to be in the very essence of a republican government. Obviously this was the opinion of the framers of the Constitution of the United States. They constituted a Senate, and constituted it in such manner as to give it, in greater or less measure, a steady control in the action of the government.

61. By the mode of their election, the members of the Senate are likely to be men of known ability and established character. By their term of office, they are in a situation to disregard those gusts of passion or delusion that frequently sweep over all communities, and can await in security the return of reason, of justice, and moderation.

How constituted.

62. The Constitution provides that the Senate shall be composed of two senators from each state, chosen by the legislature thereof for six years, and that each senator shall have one vote.

63. This equality of representation in the Senate, without reference to the disproportion in the territory, wealth, or population of the several states, was the result of compromise and mutual concession. The small states demanded it as a means of protection against the large, and as being in accordance with the federal principle: the proportional representation in the House being conformable to the national principle, and thus securing the large states against the small.

Mode of Election.

64. The members of the Senate are chosen by the legislatures of the respective states, and generally by a joint vote, that is, both branches of the legislature unite and form one assembly, and the majority elect. The Senate, however, in a recent case, decided that, in order to the validity of such an election, both branches, acting separately, must first have voted to meet as a joint body, and have actually met accordingly. In some of the states each branch gives a separate and independent vote, and a majority of each must concur in the choice of the same candidate or there is no election. This is called a concurrent vote. By the act of July 25, 1866, Congress prescribed the following mode of electing senators:—The legislature of each state which shall be chosen

next preceding the expiration of the time for which any Senator was elected to represent said state in Congress, shall, on the second Tuesday after the meeting and organization thereof, proceed to elect a Senator in Congress, in the place of such Senator so going out of office, in the following manner: Each house shall openly, by a *viva voce* of each member present, name one person for Senator in Congress from said state, and the name of the person so voted for who shall have a majority of the whole number of votes cast in each house shall be entered on the journal of each house, by the clerk or secretary thereof; but if either house shall fail to give such majority to any person on said day, that fact shall be entered on the journal. At twelve o'clock, meridian, of the day following that on which proceedings are required to take place, as aforesaid, the members of the two houses shall convene in joint assembly, and the journal of each house shall then be read, and if the same person shall have received a majority of all the votes in each house, such person shall be duly declared elected Senator to represent said state in the Congress of the United States; but if the same person shall not have received a majority of the votes in each house, or if either house shall have failed to take proceedings as required by this act, the joint assembly shall then proceed to choose, by a *viva voce* vote of each member present, a person for the purpose aforesaid; and the person having a majority of all the votes of the said joint assembly, a majority of all the members of both houses being present and voting, shall be declared duly elected; and in case no person shall receive such majority on the first day, the joint assembly shall meet at twelve o'clock meridian of each succeeding day, during the session of the legislature, and take at least one vote until a Senator shall be elected.

Elections to fill Vacancies.

Whenever, on the meeting of the legislature of any state, a vacancy shall exist in the representation of such state in the Senate of the United States, said legislature shall proceed, on the second Tuesday after the commencement and organization of its session, to elect a person to fill such vacancy, in the manner hereinbefore provided for the election of a Senator for a full term; and if a vacancy shall happen during the session of the legislature, then, on the second Tuesday after the legislature shall have been organized and shall have notice of such vacancy.

Certificates of Election.

It shall be the duty of the governor of the state from which any Senator shall have been chosen as aforesaid, to certify his election, under the seal of the state, to the President of the United States; which certificate shall be countersigned by the secretary of state of the state.

Term of Office.

65. The Senators are chosen for six years; but, as if to obviate any objection that might be urged against so long a term, the Constitution has provided that immediately after the Senate should be assembled, in consequence of the first election, they should be divided, as equally as might be, into three classes: the seats of the Senators of the first class to be vacated at the expiration of the second year; of the second class, at the expiration of the fourth year; and of the third class, at the expiration of the sixth year. Thus one-third are chosen every second year.

66. By this arrangement, while fresh members are introduced into the Senate biennially, there is a much larger number who have acquired experience and familiarity with the public business. As new states are admitted into the Union, and additional members are thus brought into the Senate, they are placed by lot in the foregoing classes, but in such manner as to keep the classes as nearly equal as possible. In arranging the classes, care was taken to place the Senators from the same state in different classes, so that their term of service should not expire at the same time, and thus leave the senatorial representation of the state vacant.

Vacancies in the Senate.

67. If vacancies happen in the Senate by resignation, or otherwise, during the recess of the legislature of any state, the executive thereof may make temporary appointments until the next meeting of the legislature, which must then fill such vacancies.

68. In one instance it was decided by the Senate that the seat of a Senator is vacated by a resignation addressed to the executive of the state, though he may have received no notice that it was accepted; and in another that the executive of a state could not make an appointment in the recess of its legislature in anticipation of a vacancy; it being held that the vacancy must actually have occurred before the appointment could legally be made.

Qualifications for a Senator.

69. As the members of the Senate are chosen differently from the members of the House, and for a longer term, so also their qualifications are different and their powers greater. No person can be a Senator who has not attained the age of thirty years, and been nine years a citizen of the United States, and who is not, when elected, an inhabitant of the state for which he is chosen.

70. When we reflect that history furnishes us with many conspicuous examples of men who have exhibited extraordinary abilities at the very outset of their career; that Hannibal, for instance, was but twenty-six when he led the Carthaginian army into Italy, Scipio but twenty-seven when entrusted with the command of the Roman legions in Spain, and Napoleon also but twenty-seven when he began his astonishing career of victory, it may, perhaps, appear singular that the Constitution should place the qualification for a Senator, in point of age, at thirty years, rather than at twenty-five, which is prescribed for a Representative. But when we consider, on the other hand, that genius and intuition are vouchsafed to but few, and that study, experience, and observation, are necessary to form most men and fit them for the discharge of important duties, the propriety of this qualification will appear. For, it may be confidently affirmed, that, except in rare instances, a person under the age of thirty will not possess that knowledge, that discipline of mind and stability of character suited to the grave position of a Senator of the United States: the duties of that position, as we shall presently see, being of a more important nature and of a wider range than those confided to a Representative.

71. It will be observed that foreigners are eligible

to the Senate after a citizenship of nine years. They become citizens upon naturalization; but they cannot become naturalized until after a previous residence of five years. Thus fourteen years must expire before a foreigner can be elected to the Senate. It will be recollected that he is eligible to the House of Representatives after a citizenship of seven years. The fact that the Senate concur with the executive in making treaties with foreign nations, suggests the reason why a too hasty admission of adopted citizens into that branch of the government might be attended with serious inconvenience, by creating a channel for foreign influence; and also the reason why the qualification, in point of citizenship, is raised higher for the Senate than for the House of Representatives.

72. The only other qualification prescribed for a Senator is, that he must when elected be an inhabitant of the state for which he is chosen. If this qualification be important, as is thought, in order that a Senator, by being an inhabitant of the state for which he is chosen, may have a more intimate knowledge of its wants, and a more sensitive regard to its rights, character, and dignity, it is singular that the Constitution should not have gone further, and required that he should continue an inhabitant of the state during his senatorial term. As it now stands, a Senator may be an inhabitant of the state

for which he is chosen on the day of his election, and cease to be an inhabitant the day after, and yet continue its representative.

73. We have now considered the qualifications attached to the office of a Senator of the United States. These qualifications, it will be observed, are confined to three particulars, and have regard only to age, citizenship, and inhabitancy. First, he must be thirty years of age; secondly, he must have been nine years a citizen of the United States; and, thirdly, he must, when elected, be an inhabitant of the state for which he is chosen.

President of the Senate.

74. The President of the Senate is the Vice-President of the United States; but he has no vote unless the Senators be equally divided. The House of Representatives choose their Speaker from among their own members; but the Vice-President is not a member of the Senate, and is not chosen as their presiding officer by themselves.

75. The reason for this difference is not very obvious: but the necessity of providing for the case of a vacancy in the office of President gave rise to the creation of the office of Vice-President, and if he were not to be President of the Senate he would be without employment.

Officers and President pro tempore.

76. With the exception of the Vice-President, the Senate choose all their other officers, and also a President *pro tempore*, in the absence of the Vice-President, or when he exercises the office of President of the United States, as he may in the cases to be mentioned hereafter. It is customary for the Vice-President, before the close of each session, to vacate the chair, in order that the Senate may choose a President *pro tempore*, who becomes their presiding officer, in case the Vice-President should, in the recess, succeed to the Presidency, in consequence of the death of the President or his resignation, or inability to discharge the powers and duties of the office.

Impeachment.

77. We have already seen that the House of Representatives possess the sole power of impeachment, and we must now add that the Senate have the sole power of trying the party accused. It would be obviously unjust to permit the accusers to try the accusation which they make; and hence it is, that the Constitution intrusts the House with the one duty and the Senate with the other.

78. This process of impeachment is borrowed from

England, where the Commons impeach, that is, make the accusation, and the Lords try; and is designed to reach public functionaries, the President, Vice-President, heads of departments, foreign ministers, judges, and all civil officers of the United States, who, in the course of their employment, are guilty of treason, bribery, or other high crimes and misdemeanors.

79. When sitting as a court of impeachment the Senate are required to be on oath or affirmation. When acting in a similar capacity the House of Lords only make a declaration upon their honor. As the members of that house cannot testify as witnesses, except on oath, there would seem to be no good reason for permitting them to act as judges without a similar obligation resting upon them. Another difference is, that two-thirds of the Senators present must concur in order to convict, whereas a majority of the Lords is sufficient for that purpose. It is necessary, however, to the validity of a judgment of impeachment that at least twelve of the Lords concur in it—a verdict by less than twelve would not be good.

80. In a trial by jury, the verdict must be unanimous, but if that principle were to be adopted in the trial of political offenders, there would be reason to fear that from political sympathy few convictions

would ever take place. And if a simple majority were sufficient there would be danger, in times of high party excitement, that the person impeached might be unjustly convicted.

81. When the President of the United States is tried, the Chief Justice of the Supreme Court presides; because the Vice-President, from a possible desire to succeed to his office, might be tempted to employ his position as President of the Senate to procure his conviction. And the Chief Justice thus presiding is a constituent member of the court, and has a right to vote as such.

Judgment in Cases of Impeachment.

82. Judgment in cases of impeachment does not extend further than to removal from office, and disqualification to hold and enjoy any office of honor, trust, or profit under the United States. The party convicted is, nevertheless, liable and subject to indictment, trial, judgment, and punishment, according to law.

83. By confining the judgment of the Senate to removal from, and disqualification to hold office under the United States, the Constitution has wisely prevented tnose excessive punishments, which political resentment, warping the sense of justice, might inflict. Politically, the offender is punished by the

judgment of the Senate: criminally, he is punished by the courts of justice according to the rules and principles of law. Thus the President, convicted of treason on impeachment before the Senate, would be removed from, and might also be disqualified to hold office under the United States. But on trial and conviction for the same offence in the courts of law he would be sentenced to death, that being the penalty.

Persons liable to Impeachment.

84. The persons liable to impeachment, as we have already observed, are the President and Vice-President, and all civil officers of the United States; and the offences for which they may be impeached are treason, bribery, or other high crimes and misdemeanors.

85. Officers of the army and navy, not being "civil officers," are not liable to impeachment. They are, however, subject to trial and punishment according to the laws and usages of war. It is thought, too, that members of Congress are not liable to impeachment, because, though members of the government, they do not derive their appointment from it, but from the states, or the people of the states.

86. Treason against the United States consists only in levying war against them, or in adhering to

their enemies, giving them aid and comfort. Bribery consists in giving or receiving a reward by any civil officer of the United States, as an inducement for acting contrary to his duty. In determining what are "high crimes and misdemeanors," resort is had to the common law.

Mode of Procedure.

87. The usual course of proceeding in a case of impeachment is substantially as follows: The House of Representatives having investigated the charges laid against the accused, and become satisfied that they are well-founded, present articles of impeachment or accusation to the Senate, who thereupon summon the party to appear on a designated day and answer.

88. If he does not appear in obedience to the summons, the Senate may try the impeachment in his absence. If he does appear, he is furnished with a copy of the articles, and time is allowed him to answer them. The House reply in writing to this answer or defence, and state their readiness to prove the charges they have preferred. The impeachment is conducted on the part of the House by a committee of managers, and counsel are allowed the accused. The trial proceeds according to the rules of law and parliamentary usage.

THE ELECTION OF SENATORS AND REPRESENTATIVES.

Power of Congress respecting.

89. The times, places, and manner of holding elections for Senators and Representatives must be prescribed in each state by the legislature thereof; but Congress may at any time by law make or alter such regulations, except as to the places of choosing Senators.

90. It is obviously important that Congress should possess the power to regulate elections in the points mentioned, in order to guard against the negligence or wilful omission of a state to make any regulation at all, as well as to secure a uniformity of election in all the states, should the want of such uniformity occasion confusion or inconvenience.

91. Until a very recent period the states were left to regulate all the particulars of elections for Senators and Representatives in their own way, without the interposition of Congress. In several of the states the Representatives were chosen by a general ticket for the whole state; in other states they were chosen singly in districts. But now, in consequence of an Act of Congress passed June 25, 1842, Repre-

sentatives are elected by districts, equal in number to the number of Representatives to which the state is entitled, and each of these districts elects one Representative. [See Act of Congress, July 14, 1862, which provides that members of the House of Representatives shall be elected by single districts.]

92. There is still, however, great diversity in the time and mode of elections. In some of the states the candidate must receive a majority of all the votes in order to be elected; in others a plurality is sufficient. In one or two of the states the choice is made *viva voce*, though generally by ballot. The times of elections, too, are very various. It should be observed that when neither the legislature of a state nor Congress have prescribed the times, places, and manner of holding elections, the executive authority of such state may, in case of a vacancy, in his writ of election, fix the time and place of election.

93. Though Congress cannot alter, or make regulations, as to the place of choosing Senators, they may prescribe the times at which the choice shall be made. The exception as to place was made because the Senators are elected by the state legislatures, whose place of meeting is always at the state capitols or seats of government, unless accidental circumstances should render it necessary for them to convene elsewhere, and of this they are the proper judges.

THE MEETING OF CONGRESS.

How often Congress must meet.

94. Congress must assemble, at least, once in every year, and such meeting must be on the first Monday in December, unless they appoint by law a different day.

95. Under the Confederation the delegates were elected annually, and assembled in Congress on the first Monday in November of every year. The state legislatures also assembled annually, and the opinion was well nigh universal among the people that the annual meeting of the legislature was not only convenient, but necessary as a check on the executive department, which, if left too long in control of public affairs without legislative supervision, might come to possess a disproportionate influence, and thus endanger the public liberty. Hence it is, that the Constitution, embodying the prevailing opinion and practice, requires Congress to assemble, at least, once in every year.

POWERS AND PRIVILEGES OF THE RESPECTIVE HOUSES.

Each House to judge of the Elections, &c.

96. Each House is the judge of the elections, returns, and qualifications of its own members, and a majority of each constitutes a quorum to do business; but a smaller number may adjourn from day to day, and may be authorized to compel the attendance of absent members, in such manner and under such penalties as each House may provide.

Contested Seats.

97. It frequently happens that there are two claimants, each asserting a right to hold the same seat in the Senate or House, as the case may be. Now it is obvious that some tribunal must be clothed with the power to decide between them, to investigate the facts, and ascertain which one of them is the rightful claimant. This power might have been vested in the Supreme Court; but it was thought best to confide it directly to each house of Congress. The decision of the House is final and conclusive.

98. If the executive of the state should refuse to grant a certificate of election, this, according to one

decision of the House, would not prejudice the right of the person entitled to a seat; nor, on the other hand, would a certificate of election be conclusive upon the House. In either case it may examine other evidence, and decide according to the weight and nature of the proofs.

Quorum.

99. Neither house can transact business without a majority of the members being present. The Constitution has wisely established this rule, and thus rendered it impossible for laws to be passed by stealth or surprise, and in opposition to the opinions of the majority of the House. But a smaller number may adjourn from day to day, and may be authorized to compel the attendance of absent members. By the rules of the House of Representatives, any fifteen members (including the Speaker, if there be one) may compel the attendance of absent members. Thus a dissolution of either house is guarded against, and a quorum at the same time insured.

Rules of Proceeding, &c.

100. Each House may determine the rules of its proceedings, punish its members for disorderly behavior, and, with the concurrence of two-thirds, expel a member.

101. The ordinary course of proceeding in Congress, under the rules established by the respective Houses, is as follows: One day's notice of a motion for leave to bring in a bill, in cases of a general nature, is required. Every bill must have three readings previous to its being passed, and these readings must be on different days, and no bill can be committed or amended until it has been twice read. The object of these forms is, to guard against surprise or imposition. In the House of Representatives, bills, after being twice read, are committed to a committee of the whole house, when the Speaker leaves the chair and takes part, if he chooses, in the debate as an ordinary member, and a chairman is appointed in his stead.

102. When a bill has passed one House it is transmitted to the other, and goes through a similar form; though in the Senate there is less formality, and bills are often committed to a select committee, chosen by ballot. If a bill be altered or amended in the House to which it is transmitted, it is then returned to the House in which it originated, and if the two Houses cannot agree, they appoint committees to confer together on the subject. When a bill is engrossed, and has passed both Houses, it is transmitted to the President for his sanction.

Punishment of Members.

103. It has been contended that the Constitution only confers on each House of Congress the power to punish its members for disorderly behavior during the session of the House, and within its presence. But the prevailing opinion is, that members may be punished for disorderly behavior committed during the session of Congress, no matter whether it be committed within or without the walls of the House; and that a member may be expelled for any misdemeanor inconsistent with his trust and duty, no matter whether he commits the misdemeanor during the session of Congress or otherwise, nor whether such misdemeanor is punishable by statute or not.

104. Each House of Congress not only possesses this express power of punishing its own members, but the implied power of protecting itself from injury or insult on the part of others; or, in other words, of punishing for any contempts committed against itself. This power of punishment is deemed essential to the dignity, safety, and self-protection of a deliberative assembly.

105. The extent to which it may be carried has been a subject of grave discussion, and the conclusion arrived at is, that it is limited to imprisonment, which must terminate with the adjournment of Congress. For although the legislative power continues per-

petual, the legislative body ceases to exist at the moment of its adjournment or periodical dissolution.

The Journal of Proceedings.

106. Each House must keep a journal of its proceedings, and, from time to time, publish the same, excepting such parts as may, in their judgment, require secrecy; and the yeas and nays of the members of either House, on any question, must, at the desire of one-fifth of those present, be entered on the journal.

107. A journal preserves in permanent form a record of the proceedings of Congress, and its publication, from time to time, insures to the people authentic information of their official acts. As the proceedings of Congress, however, are generally conducted in public, and immediately communicated to the people through the press, and in advance of the official publication of their journal, this provision of the Constitution may, on a first view, seem to be needless. But when we consider that neither House is required to sit with open doors, and might, if they chose, conduct all their proceedings in secret, as was done by the Senate at the outset of the government, the importance of this provision for the publication of their journal will appear.

108. When business of a confidential nature is

brought before either House, all persons are excluded but their officers. The Senate, too, holds what are termed "Executive Sessions," in which confidential communications from the President are considered, such as nominations to office, treaties, &c. The journal of its proceedings on occasions of this kind, unless the injunction of secrecy has been removed, is not made public, but is kept in a distinct record, which is only accessible to certain privileged persons.

The Yeas and Nays.

109. The importance of that portion of the clause which requires the yeas and nays to be entered on the journal, if one-fifth of the members present desire it, is obvious. By this means the people know how their representatives vote, and thus caution and deliberation are induced on the part of the latter. As too much time, however, would be consumed in calling the yeas and nays on every question, and as they might be called by factious or dissatisfied members for the sole purpose of delaying and embarrassing the passage of measures, it is wisely provided that they shall not be called, or entered upon the journal, unless at the desire of one-fifth of the members present.

Adjournments.

110. Neither House, during the session of Congress, can, without the consent of the other, adjourn

for more than three days, nor to any other place than that in which the two Houses shall be sitting.

111. This clause was intended to prevent either House from interrupting the regular course of legislation by undue adjournments. In this particular they are restrained both as to time and place. In case of disagreement between them, with respect to the time of adjournment, the President may adjourn them to such time as he shall think proper. With this exception, the executive department has nothing whatever to do with the duration or the adjournment of Congress. In England, on the contrary, the King may prorogue or dissolve Parliament at his pleasure.

Duration of Congress.

112. It will be recollected that the members of the House are chosen for two years, and also that the seats of one-third of the Senators become vacant every second year. Hence the duration of each Congress is two years. And as the Constitution requires them to assemble at least once in every year, it follows that each Congress will necessarily hold not less than two sessions. In addition to these, the President is empowered, on extraordinary occasions, to convene both Houses, or either of them.

PRIVILEGES AND DISABILITIES OF MEMBERS.

Compensation.

113. The Senators and Representatives receive a compensation for their services, ascertained by law, and paid out of the Treasury of the United States.

114. In England, the members of Parliament receive no compensation; their services being considered merely honorary. It seems, however, to harmonize best with the genius of a republican government to adopt the contrary practice. Without compensation an undue advantage would be given to the rich. Men of talents, who were not favored by fortune, might be deterred from seeking or accepting a position whose expenses they could ill support. And, if they did obtain a seat in the national councils, their necessities might expose them to pecuniary temptations.

115. The Congress of the Confederation were paid by their respective states; but the Senators and Representatives under the Constitution are paid out of the Treasury of the United States—the amount being determined by an act of Congress. Under the first

system it was thought the members of Congress were too much the mere agents and advocates of state interests, instead of being the impartial umpires and guardians of justice and the general good. To avoid this evil, to prevent too much dependence on the states, the Constitution changed the mode of payment from the states to the United States.

Freedom from Arrest.

116. The Senators and Representatives are, in all cases, except treason, felony, and breach of the peace, privileged from arrest during their attendance at the session of their respective Houses, and in going to, and returning from, the same. And, for any speech or debate in either House they are not to be questioned in any other place.

117. The privilege of members of Congress from arrest, except for the offences mentioned in the preceding section, is founded upon important public reasons. They are exempted while going, because it is necessary that they should reach the scene of their labors; they are exempted while there, because if they could be withdrawn from their seats at the suit of creditors, or by any other merely civil process, such as a summons to testify as witnesses, or to serve as jurors, the voice of their constituents would be lost, and the public interests, perhaps, suffer

serious inconvenience; they are exempted while returning, because, having gone from home in the service of the public, it is proper that the public should insure their return to it safe from interruption.

118. It has also been held that this privilege from arrest extends to one duly commissioned as a member, though Congress should decide, upon investigation, that he is not entitled to a seat. In going and returning a member is not restricted to a precise number of days, but the law allows him a reasonable time. Nor is he restricted to the most direct route, and any little deviation from it will be presumed to have been directed by some superior convenience or necessity. Neither does the law compel him to set out on his return immediately upon the adjournment; but allows him time to settle his private affairs, and to prepare for his journey.

119. If the immunity from arrest is disregarded, the member thus unlawfully arrested will at once be discharged on application to a court of justice. He may also maintain an action against the party making the arrest, or procure his indictment for the trespass. The aggressor may also be punished by the House for contempt. But the privileges of a member are not so extensive that his suits cannot be forced to a trial and decision while the session of Congress continues. While privileged from arrests both on judicial and mesne process, and from the

service of a summons or other civil process while in attendance on their public duties, none of the reasons on which this privilege is allowed can extend it to the right to continue a cause pending in court.

Immunity of Debate.

120. For any speech or debate in either house, the members are not to be questioned in any other place. The object of this clause is to secure the utmost freedom in the discussion of public measures. It is a moot question, however, whether a member, who publishes his speech which contains libellous matter, is liable to an action and prosecution therefor, as in common cases of libel? Though a member may not be questioned elsewhere for any slander he may utter in debate, it is contended that the publication of such slander is an independent act, not at all connected with the discharge of his duties, and not protected by the privilege granted him by the Constitution. But where Congress direct the publication of their debates, as is at present the case, the responsibility of the individual member would seem clearly to cease, because the publication of his speech is not his act, but the act of the body to which he belongs.

Disability to hold Office.

121. No Senator or Representative can, during the time for which he was elected, be appointed to

any civil office under the authority of the United States, which has been created, or the emoluments whereof have been increased, during such time. And no person, holding any office under the United States, can be a member of either House of Congress during his continuance in office.

122. It was intended by the first part of this clause to prevent Congress from creating new offices or increasing the emoluments of old ones from personal considerations; and by the second part to guard against improper bias on the part of its members. Hence, a member of Congress appointed to an office under the United States, must resign his seat. If he accepts the office without such resignation, it operates as a forfeiture of his seat. On the other hand, an officer of the United States, if elected a member of Congress, must resign his office, though his continuing to execute its duties after his election does not operate as a disqualification; it only being necessary that he should resign his office prior to taking his seat. In other words, a person cannot at the same time be a member of Congress and hold office under the United States. The acceptance of a military commission in a volunteer regiment, mustered into the service of the United States, operates as a forfeiture of his seat.

THE PASSAGE OF LAWS.

The Initiative of Revenue Bills.

123. All bills for raising revenue must originate in the House of Representatives; but the Senate may propose or concur with amendments, as on other bills.

124. It was thought that the House of Representatives, being more popular in its character, more immediately dependent on the people, and likely to possess more extensive local information than the Senate, was the fittest body to be intrusted with the initiative in the imposition of taxes. Under the English system the Commons originate money bills, and the Lords simply approve or reject. Unlike our Senate, they have no power to alter or amend.

125. By bills for raising revenue are meant bills to levy taxes in the usual sense of the word; and not bills for other purposes, though they may incidentally create revenue.

The Veto Power.

126. Every bill which has passed the House of Representatives and the Senate must, before it becomes a law, be presented to the President of the

United States; if he approves he must sign it, but if not he must return it with his objections to the House in which it originated, who must enter the objections at large on their journal, and proceed to reconsider it. If after such reconsideration two-thirds of that House agree to pass the bill, it must be sent, together with the objections, to the other House, by which it must likewise be reconsidered, and if approved by two-thirds of that House it becomes a law. But in all such cases the votes of both Houses must be determined by yeas and nays, and the names of the persons voting for or against the bill be entered on the journal of each House respectively. If any bill is not returned by the President within ten days (Sundays excepted) after having been presented to him, it becomes a law, in like manner as if he had signed it, unless the Congress, by their adjournment, prevent its return, in which case it does not become a law.

127. The power with which the President is invested of objecting to the passage of a bill is called the veto power; and both the word and the power are derived from the Romans. The word itself means *I forbid*, and was used by the tribunes of the people to hinder the passage of any obnoxious decree of the senate. The object of placing this power in the hands of the President is to secure the authority

confided to the executive department from encroachment, and also to interpose another check against hasty or improvident legislation. But, in order to prevent an abuse of the power, it is provided that two-thirds of both Houses, that is, two-thirds of a quorum of each House, may pass a bill notwithstanding his veto. His returning a bill, with the reasons and arguments that induced him to return it, is not an absolute defeat of the bill, but an appeal, as it were, to the legislature to reconsider it.

Joint Orders, Resolutions, &c.

128. Not only must every bill which has passed the House and Senate be presented to the President for his approval or rejection, but every order, resolution, or vote to which the concurrence of both Houses is necessary, except on a question of adjournment. And before the same can take effect it must be approved by him, or, being disapproved, must be repassed by two-thirds of the Senate and House of Representatives, according to the rules and limitations prescribed in the case of a bill.

129. The object of thus extending the veto power is to prevent Congress from evading the President's negative by passing laws in the form of an order or resolution instead of a bill. This does not apply, however, to orders, resolutions, or votes to which the

concurrence of both Houses is not necessary. But separate resolutions of either House of Congress, except in matters appertaining to their own parliamentary rights, have no legal effect to constrain the action of the President or heads of departments.

130. When a bill has been passed by Congress it is enrolled on parchment of uniform size and signed by the Speaker of the House of Representatives and the President of the Senate. It is then sent to the President of the United States, and if approved and signed by him he notifies Congress of the fact, and deposits the original in the office of the Secretary of State. Every bill operates as a law from the time when it is approved by the President, and is prospective in its effect only. The legal fiction that there is no fraction of a day is not applicable in such a case.

THE POWERS OF CONGRESS.

Taxation.

131. We have now arrived at that part of the Constitution which has given rise to much discussion, and with regard to which opinions have been greatly divided. In treating upon it we shall endeavor to confine ourselves within the limits marked out by the well-settled practice of the government, and the authoritative exposition of the courts.

132. Congress have power to lay and collect taxes, duties, imposts, and excises, to pay the debts, and provide for the common defence and general welfare of the United States; but all duties, imposts, and excises must be uniform throughout the United States.

133. This clause of the Constitution has been a subject of much controversy. On one hand it has been said that it empowers Congress to lay and collect taxes, duties, imposts, and excises, *and also* to pay the debts and provide for the common defence and general welfare of the United States. On the other it is contended that Congress is empowered to lay and collect taxes, duties, imposts, and excises,

for the purpose of paying the debts and providing for the common defence and general welfare. The latter is the common, and doubtless correct interpretation. The power to tax is not, therefore, a distinct and unlimited power; but is restrained to the payment of the debts, and provision for the common defence and general welfare of the United States. Moreover, Congress cannot tax the means and instrumentalities by which the states carry on the operations of their respective governments. They cannot tax its judicial process, nor the salaries of its officers, nor require a stamp upon the official bonds of state officers. This exemption arises from implication, and rests upon the law of self-preservation. If the means employed by a state government in conducting its operations could be taxed at discretion by the general government, the former would exist at the mercy of the latter. On the other hand, as we shall see hereafter, the instrumentalities of the general government are equally exempt from the influence of state taxation. But it is only property exempt from taxation by the Constitution that is beyond the taxing power of the states. Congress has no power to exempt other property from such taxation.

Different Kinds of Taxes.

134. Taxes are commonly designated as direct or indirect, according to their character, and are imposed

by the government for the service of the state. Direct taxes are laid directly on land or real property, or upon persons, in which case they are spoken of as personal, poll, or capitation taxes. Indirect taxes are laid on articles of consumption, whether those articles consist of imports or manufactures. In this description of tax are included duties, imposts, and excises. By duties are generally meant taxes upon goods, imported or exported, though, as we shall see hereafter, the Constitution inhibits a tax or duty on articles exported from any state. Imposts, in a restricted sense, mean taxes on goods imported from abroad. Excise is an inland tax levied upon various commodities of home use or consumption, usually while in the hands of the producer or manufacturer.

Rule by which Taxes are levied.

135. All duties, imposts, and excises, must be uniform throughout the United States; but a different rule is prescribed for capitation or other direct taxes. These must be levied, not according to the rule of uniformity, but according to the rule of apportionment, that is, they must be apportioned among the several states, according to their respective numbers.

136. A case decided by the Supreme Court soon after the organization of the government, furnishes a

very good illustration of the difference between the rule which requires that direct taxes shall be apportioned among the states according to their respective numbers, and the rule which requires that duties, imposts, and excises, shall be uniform throughout the United States. It arose as follows :—By an Act of Congress, passed in 1794, a duty of ten dollars each *per annum* was laid on carriages, and the levy made uniform throughout the United States, that is, each owner of a carriage was to pay ten dollars *per annum*, no matter whether the number of such owners in a particular state was few or many. The constitutionality of the act was contested upon the ground that it was a direct tax, and hence should be *apportioned* among the states according to their numbers.

137. In this case, the proportion of tax awarded to a particular state, determined by its numbers, might be two hundred dollars, and yet there might not be more than two carriages in that state. Hence, although Congress only intended to lay a tax of ten dollars on each carriage, the owners of the two carriages would be compelled to pay one hundred dollars each. The Supreme Court, however, decided that the carriage tax was not a direct tax in the sense of the Constitution, and hence should be levied as Congress had directed according to the rule of uniformity. In addition to the fact that direct taxes were

supposed to have reference only to land and persons, this consideration was decisive with the court, namely, that no tax could be a direct tax in the sense of the Constitution which was incapable of apportionment according to the constitutional rule. And, if in any one of the states there should be no carriages, then there could be no apportionment at all.

Taxes may be extended to the Territories, &c.

138. The power to levy and collect taxes, duties, imposts, and excises, is coextensive with the territory of the United States. Hence Congress, in laying a direct tax, may extend it to the District of Columbia and the territories. If this be done, the same rule which is applied to the states must be applied to them, namely, the rule of apportionment. It is equally necessary too that uniformity in the imposition of imposts, duties, and excises, should be observed in the one as in the other.

Power to borrow Money.

139. Congress have not only the power to raise money by means of taxes, duties, imposts, and excises, but the power to borrow money on the credit of the United States—a power absolutely necessary in order that provision may be made for those exigencies which arise in time of war, and those extra-

ordinary and unexpected demands on the treasury which occasionally occur in time of peace. And the states have no power to tax the loans thus made.

Commerce.

140. Among the more prominent defects of the Articles of Confederation was the want of a general authority over commerce. This induced injurious regulations on the part of foreign nations, from their knowledge that Congress had no power to adopt countervailing measures, and also led to most irritating and complicating regulations on the part of the several states. Subjected to this double pressure, the commerce of the country was at a stand, and the union and harmony of the states were fast giving way to mutual discord and hatred. The evil was great and pressing, and was one of the chief causes that conduced to the call of the Federal Convention and the establishment of the Constitution. Hence, it was provided that Congress should have power to regulate commerce with foreign nations, and among the several states, and with the Indian tribes.

141. To regulate commerce is to prescribe the rule by which commerce is to be governed. Commerce with foreign nations and among the several states, means intercourse with those nations, and among those states, for the purposes of trade, be the object

of the trade what it may; and this intercourse includes all the means by which it can be carried on, whether by the free navigation of the waters of the several states, or by a passage over land through the states, when such passage becomes necessary to the commercial intercourse between the states.

142. Commerce *among* the several states means commerce which concerns more states than one. It does not comprehend any commerce which is purely internal, between man and man in a single state, or between different parts of the same state, and not extending to or affecting other states. At the same time commerce among the states does not stop at the external boundary line of each state, but may be introduced into the interior. The word *among* means intermingled with.

143. The power to regulate commerce may be variously applied, as, for example, by laws for the regulation of the coasting trade and fisheries, and wrecks of the sea, and for the punishment of crimes upon stranded vessels; for the government of seamen on board of American ships, and the imposition of embargoes; for the construction of light-houses and buoys, the removal of obstructions to navigation in rivers, bays, lakes, and harbors; the imposition of duties upon articles of importation; the designation of particular ports of entry and delivery, and for

conferring privileges upon ships built and owned in the United States.

144. While it has been held that the power to regulate commerce is exclusive, so that the states cannot legislate upon the same subject, it has been equally held that they may enact police regulations, although such regulations operate on the agents and subjects of commerce, restricted only by this limitation, that in the event of collision, the law of the state must yield to that of Congress. Thus the states may pass license laws restricting the sale of spirituous liquors imported either from foreign countries or the other states of the Union; and inspection and quarantine laws which delay the landing of ships and cargoes, and also laws for the removal or destruction of unsound and infectious articles which have been imported, and laws regulating pilots and to protect their fisheries. Because the right of Congress to regulate commerce necessarily contemplates limitations and exceptions in favor of the states, in cases affecting the morals, health, or safety of the community.

145. The states may pass laws, too, requiring the master of every vessel arriving in one of their ports to make a report, in writing, respecting his passengers, and to give a bond indemnifying the authorities of the port from all expenses and charges which may

be incurred in the maintenance of all such passengers who are not citizens of the United States; and also requiring him, on the order of such authorities, to remove to the place of his last settlement, any passenger, being a citizen of the United States, who should be likely to become chargeable on the public. Such laws are deemed police regulations, and not regulations of commerce, and are passed with a view to prevent the citizens of a state from being oppressed by the support of multitudes of poor persons, who come from foreign countries without possessing the means of supporting themselves.

146. But the states cannot pass laws imposing a tax upon passengers, either foreigners or citizens, coming into their ports, either in foreign vessels or vessels of the United States, from foreign nations or the other states of the Union: such laws are unconstitutional and void, being, in their nature, regulations of commerce: and the commerce of the United States includes an intercourse of persons as well as the importation of merchandise. The states, therefore, cannot tax the one any more than the other. Nor can they require an importer to take out a license and pay therefor before selling a package of imported goods. But they may impose a tax on brokers dealing in foreign exchange, and also a tax on legacies payable to aliens. And after the introduction of imported goods or imported liquors into a state, and the

original packages are broken up for use or retail by the importer, or by a purchaser from him, even though still in the original packages, then they become subject to the laws of the state, and may be taxed for state purposes, and the sale regulated by state laws.

147. The power of Congress to regulate commerce extends to the Indian tribes, no matter whether they live within or without the boundaries of particular states. In the exercise of this power Congress may prohibit all intercourse with them, except under a license. The Indian tribes are not regarded as foreign nations in the sense of the Constitution, and as such entitled to sue in the courts of the United States; but as domestic dependent nations.

Naturalization and Bankruptcy.

148. The next power intrusted to Congress is, to establish a uniform rule of naturalization; and uniform laws on the subject of bankruptcies throughout the United States.

149. Naturalization is the investing of foreigners with the privileges of native citizens. The rule for doing this should be uniform, because the citizens of one state are entitled to all the rights of citizenship in every other state. Hence, if the several states could adopt dissimilar rules, it would follow that any one state could render nugatory the rules of all the

rest. For by naturalizing aliens upon easy conditions, it would enable them to pass into the other states and enjoy all the rights of citizenship, in spite of their policy and laws. It was to guard against an anomaly like this that the power was confided to Congress of establishing a uniform rule of naturalization throughout the United States, and this power must necessarily be exclusive.

150. The rule actually established by Congress requires a previous residence of five years before an alien can become a citizen of the United States. The steps he must take, in order to be clothed with this character, are few and simple. He must first declare, on oath or affirmation, before a state or United States court, his intention to become a citizen of the United States, and to renounce all allegiance to the government of which he is at the time a subject. This declaration must be made at least two years before his application for admission as a citizen. When this latter application is made he must declare, on oath or affirmation, that he will support the Constitution of the United States, and that he doth renounce and abjure all allegiance and fidelity to every foreign prince or state; and in case he shall have borne any hereditary title, or have been of any of the orders of nobility in the kingdom or state from which he came, he must make an express renunciation of such title or order of nobility.

151. As we have before remarked, he must have resided in the United States five years at least prior to his application, and in the state or territory where he then resides, at least one year, and during that time have behaved as a man of good moral character, attached to the principles of the Constitution of the United States, and well-disposed to the good order and happiness of the same. His residence and good moral character must be proved in court by the testimony of witnesses; the oath of the applicant being in no case allowed to prove his residence.

151½. Congress, by the act of July 27, 1868, formally committed the government of the United States to the support of the doctrine of expatriation, in opposition to the English common law principle that allegiance is intrinsic and perpetual. In that act Congress has assumed and declared that the right of expatriation is a natural and inherent right of all people, indispensable to the enjoyment of the rights of life, liberty, and the pursuit of happiness; and declared inconsistent with the fundamental principles of the government any declaration, instruction, opinion, order or decision of any officers thereof which denies, restricts, impairs or questions the right of expatriation; and moreover, that the naturalized citizen, while in foreign states, is entitled to, and shall receive, the same protection of person and property that is accorded to the native-born citizen in the same situation and circumstances.

Bankrupt Laws.

152. A bankrupt law may be defined as a law which discharges a debtor from the legal obligation to pay his debts in such cases and upon such condition as the law may specify—the usual condition being that he shall surrender all his property to commissioners for the benefit of his creditors. The English bankrupt laws relate to merchants and traders; but such laws may equally be made to embrace every description of debtors, as the bankrupt laws of the United States have done.

153. The power to pass uniform laws on the subject of bankruptcies, Congress have, for the most part, permitted to lie dormant. An act of this kind was passed in 1801, but was repealed two years subsequently; and the act of 1842 was repealed at the very next session of Congress. Meanwhile, several of the states have passed laws of this character—it being held that so long as Congress abstains from exercising the power it possesses over the subject, the states may exercise it, but with this limitation, namely, that the laws passed by the states cannot discharge contracts made *prior* to their passage, and only such contracts as are made within their respective states and between citizens of the same. When Congress, too, exercises its power and

passes a uniform bankrupt law, the laws of the several states upon the same subject yield to it and become inoperative. Accordingly, the act of March 2, 1867, generally known as the Bankrupt Act, suspended, *ipso facto,* all action upon future cases arising under the insolvency laws of the states, where such laws act upon the same subject-matter and the same persons as the act of Congress.

Coinage of Money, &c.

154. Congress have power to coin money, regulate the value thereof, and of foreign coin, and fix the standard of weights and measures.

155. Uniformity in the value of money is vastly important in a country like ours, composed of a great number of states whose intercourse should be freed, as much as possible, from all embarrassment arising from an uncertain and variable currency. Hence the propriety of giving to Congress the power to secure such uniformity by coining money and regulating its value, as well as the value of foreign coin. From the power of coining and regulating the metallic currency Congress has, in part, derived the right of issuing paper, to circulate as its representative. And after the breaking out of the civil war in 1861, Congress, by what are familiarly known as the legal tender acts, made its paper issues a legal tender in payment of private debts, as well as of all public dues except

duties on imports and interest on the public debt. In other words, Congress made its paper currency, in the payment of private debts and most of the public dues, equivalent to the metallic currency, however great the nominal disproportion. The constitutionality of these acts was strongly contested; but they were finally sustained by the Supreme Court of the United States, both in their application to pre-existing and subsequently contracted debts.

156. Money is coined at the Mint of the United States, which was established in 1792, at Philadelphia, where it has since been continued. There have been established also, at different times, branch mints in North Carolina, Georgia, Louisiana, and California.

157. The power to fix the standard of weights and measures Congress has not yet thought proper to exercise. Accordingly the several states, in the absence of a uniform law upon the subject, have continued to use either the standards which existed when the Constitution was adopted, or other standards which the convenience of commerce has led them to adopt since. But by the act of July 28, 1873, Congress made it lawful throughout the United States to employ the weights and measures of the metric system; and no contract or dealing, or pleading in any court, can be deemed invalid or liable to objection, because the weights or measures expressed or referred to therein are weights or measures of that system.

Power to punish Counterfeiting.

158. To render more efficient the powers to coin and borrow money, Congress are empowered to provide for the punishment of counterfeiting the securities and current coin of the United States.

159. Congress accordingly have passed several acts, imposing very severe penalties upon those who produce a false representation of the coin of the United States. It has been thought, however, that Congress could not punish for the circulation of such coin, though the states might; that is, the power of Congress has been supposed to be confined to the punishing of the offence of making counterfeit coin, the states alone possessing the power of punishing for passing it. But by recent acts, Congress has provided for the punishment as well for passing as counterfeiting the coins and securities of the United States; and no decision of the judicial tribunals has yet called in question the constitutional validity of these acts. And there seems no good reason why, on the other hand, the states may not concurrently provide for the punishment of counterfeiting; such legislation being in aid of the power of Congress.

Post-offices and Post-roads.

160. Congress have power to establish post-offices and post-roads.

161. In the first year of Washington's administration there were but twenty-five post-offices in all the United States. In the following year the income of the Post-office Department did not reach thirty-eight thousand dollars. Its income and expenditure are now reckoned by millions, and there is scarcely any portion of our immense territory, however remote, that is not visited by the mail. Intercourse between all parts of the country is thus facilitated, knowledge diffused, and the operations of government carried on with promptitude and regularity.

162. In the exercise of the power to establish post-offices and post-roads, Congress have felt themselves authorized to create the whole system appropriate to a post-office establishment. They have passed laws for the punishment of those who steal letters from the post-office, or rob the mail; they have purchased or erected buildings for post-offices, and, in some instances, laid out and made roads for the carrying of the mail, though generally they have merely designated or selected as post-roads such roads as already existed. By an Act of Congress, passed in 1853, all railroads in the United States have been declared post-roads.

163. The general control and supervision of the Post-office establishment are confided to the Postmaster-General, who is a member of the President's

Cabinet. He is authorized to establish post-offices, appoint all postmasters whose annual commissions are less than a thousand dollars, make contracts for the carriage of the mails, and direct generally the operations and affairs of the department over which he presides.

Science and Useful Arts.

164. Congress have power to promote the progress of science and the useful arts, by securing, for limited times, to authors and inventors, the exclusive right to their respective writings and discoveries.

165. In the United States an author has no exclusive property in a published work, except under some act of Congress. Such property is not recognised by the common law. In pursuance of the power confided to them by the Constitution, Congress have passed laws giving to authors, who are citizens of the United States or resident therein, the exclusive right to publish their works for a term of twenty-eight years, with the privilege of enjoying the same right for an additional period of fourteen years.

Copyrights.

166. This exclusive right of authors is called a copyright, and is granted not only to the authors of books, but to the authors of maps, charts, and mu-

sical compositions, and to the inventors and designers of prints, cuts, and engravings. If an author, inventor, designer, or engraver should not be living at the expiration of the first period of twenty-eight years, the privilege of renewal for the further period of fourteen years survives to his widow and children.

Patents.

167. The inventors or discoverers of any new and useful art, machine, manufacture, or composition of matter, or any new and useful improvement on any art, machine, manufacture, or composition of matter, not known or used by others before their discovery or invention thereof, and which has not been abandoned to the public or been in public use, or on sale, for more than two years prior to the application for a patent, are entitled to the exclusive right of manufacturing and selling such invention for the period of fourteen years. This privilege is termed a patent-right, and may, when the inventor, without neglect or fault on his part, has not been adequately remunerated, be extended for an additional period of seven years.

167½. As patents are granted "to promote the progress of science and the useful arts," the courts give them a liberal construction. Moreover, the power of Congress over them is plenary ; so that, if they do not take away the rights of property in existing patents, they may modify them; they may make special grants and special extensions; and they may also give a retrospective effect to their grants.

Piracies and Felonies.

168. To Congress is intrusted the power to define and punish piracies and felonies committed on the high seas, and offences against the law of nations.

169. Piracy is a crime well known to the law of nations, and is robbery or forcible depredations upon the sea, *animo furandi*, in the spirit and intention of universal hostility. The object of the Constitution is not, therefore, to authorize Congress to define a crime already well and universally defined, but to empower them to enumerate such crimes as shall be deemed piracies. Congress have accordingly declared the slave trade piracy, as well as every offence committed at sea, which would be punishable with death if committed on land.

170. Felony, in a general sense, is every description of crime which the common law punishes either with death or forfeiture of lands and goods. It is a term, as has been justly remarked, of loose signification in the common law, and more vague still in the law of the sea. Hence the propriety of giving Congress the power to define as well as to punish it. By

the "high seas" is meant the unenclosed waters of the ocean beyond low water mark.

171. By the law of nations is meant that system of principles and usages which regulates the intercourse of nations. Among the more obvious offences against that law may be mentioned the violation of passports, infringement of the rights of ambassadors, and the infraction of treaties. Under the Confederation Congress possessed no power to punish such offences, and were compelled to appeal to the states to provide adequate and exemplary punishment in all that class of cases. As the general government represents the country in its external relations, and is bound by the law of nations, it is wisely intrusted with the power to define offences against that law, and punish its citizens for committing them.

War.

172. Congress possess the power to declare war, grant letters of marque and reprisal, and make rules concerning captures on land and water.

173. In the ancient republics of Greece the right of declaring war resided with the assemblies of the people, who exercised a large portion of the sovereign power. In the aristocratic republic of Carthage it was confided to the senate; in Rome to the *comitia*, or assembly of the people. In the monarchies of

modern Europe the king alone declares war; but this prerogative is greatly modified in England, where the crown may indeed declare war, but cannot raise a dollar with which to carry it on without the consent of Parliament. The result is, that the real power resides in Parliament, because the crown never would venture upon a declaration of war without being sure of their support and approval. For why declare war in opposition to the views of Parliament, when it possesses the power to nullify the declaration by withholding the supplies necessary to give it effect?

174. The Constitution of the United States has not thus separated the real and nominal authority, but has given directly to Congress both the power to declare war, and, as we shall presently see, the power to provide the means to carry it on. The check to a wanton and unnecessary exercise of this power is two-fold: first, the virtue of Congress, and, secondly, their responsibility to the people. With one-third of the Senate and the whole of the House of Representatives to be elected every second year, it may well be presumed that Congress will not declare war except upon grounds that will justify them before the tribunal of public opinion.

174½. The power to declare war is exclusive in Congress, and necessarily involves the power to prosecute it by all means and in all modes known and recognized in legitimate warfare. Hence it includes the right to seize and confiscate the property of the enemy, and to acquire territory, either by conquest or by treaty. And when the authority of the United States is resisted by combinations of its citizens too strong for the civil arm of the government, it may assume the attitude of a belligerent, without relinquishing its character of a sovereign, and may enforce its rights in both capacities. But it cannot, in prosecuting its belligerent and sovereign rights against a rebellion of its citizens, create a military department out of one or more states not included in the circle of rebellion, and authorize the military commander within such department to arrest a citizen of such state, and try him before a military commission for an alleged crime. The Constitution secures to the citizen a trial by jury, and in states which have upheld the government, and where the courts are open and their process unobstructed, he cannot be held to answer for a capital or other infamous crime, unless on presentment of a grand jury, except in cases arising in the land or naval forces, or in the militia when in actual service in time of war or public danger, nor be deprived of life, liberty, or property without due process of law. And due process of law in such a case does not mean a court-martial.

Letters of Marque and Reprisal.

175. Letters of marque and reprisal are commissions or letters which authorize the persons to whom they are granted to capture the property of a foreign state, particularly its merchant vessels. They are usually granted in a time of war, and as a means to distress the enemy. They are also occasionally granted in peace, as, for example, when a nation has been injured in its own rights, or in those of its subjects, without being able to obtain justice from the tribunals or sovereign of the country against which they are issued.

176. Before private letters of marque are granted, proof must be produced of the amount of injury which has been sustained, which is set forth in the letters, in order that the surplus of property captured may, after the payment of damages, interest, and expenses, be restored to the owners. Hence all vessels seized under those letters must be brought into some port, and condemned and sold by the order of a competent court in order that the surplus, if any, may be thus restored.

177. The general principles relating to land and maritime captures are defined by the law of nations; but the rules respecting the division of the captured property, and many other details, each government

regulates for itself. Congress, as an encouragement and reward of valor, have established a rule that when a captured ship is of equal or superior force to the ship making the capture, she shall be the sole property of the captors. In all other cases the property is divided equally between the captors and the United States.

The Army.

178. As we have already remarked, the power is confided to Congress to raise and support armies; but no appropriation of money to that use can be for a longer term than two years.

179. The appropriation is confined to two years, in order to prevent the keeping on foot a standing army without the continued consent of the Representatives of the people. The actual practice is, to make the appropriations not even for two years, but only for the current year.

180. There is no restriction upon the power of Congress in raising armies as to the persons they will enlist. Hence they may enlist minors in the army or navy, without the consent of their parents. Public policy requires that a minor should be at liberty to enter into a contract to serve the state, whenever such contract is not positively forbidden by the state itself. But an Act of Congress directs

that no person under the age of eighteen shall be mustered into the United States service.

The Navy.

181. Congress are also empowered to provide and maintain a navy.

182. Congress possessed the same power under the Confederation, but were never able, from want of means, to build and equip a navy. It was not until some years after the adoption of the Constitution, and the organization of the government, that the foundation of a navy was laid. In 1797 three frigates were completed, and were named the Constitution, the United States, and the Constellation. These vessels were the germ, as it were, of our present naval force.

Government of the Army and Navy.

183. With the power to raise armies and provide a navy is associated the necessary power to make rules for the government and regulation of the land and naval forces.

The Militia.

184. Congress have also the authority to provide for calling forth the militia to execute the laws of the Union, suppress insurrections, and repel invasions.

185. By militia are meant that body of citizens in a state who are enrolled and trained to military exercises. They are a very different force from a standing army—being simply citizens who are liable to do military duty, who are regularly enrolled for that purpose, and who assemble occasionally to be taught military duties.

186. By an Act of Congress, passed in 1795, the President is authorized, in certain exigencies, such as invasion, or imminent danger of it, to call forth such number of the militia most convenient to the scene of action as he may judge necessary. It belongs to him exclusively to judge whether the exigency has actually arisen, and his decision is conclusive upon the state authorities.

187. When the militia are called into the service of the United States, and are mustered at the place of rendezvous, they cease to be state militia, and become national militia; and from that time they are paid by the United States, and are subject to the articles of war. If they neglect or refuse to march to the place of rendezvous they may be tried and fined by a court-martial, constituted under the authority of the United States, but composed of militia officers only. The states may also pass laws providing for the trial of such delinquents by court-martial. And they may employ their own militia, not called into the service of the Union, to aid the govern-

ment in executing the laws, in suppressing insurrections, and in repelling invasions.

188. Congress is not only authorized to provide for calling forth the militia, but also to provide for organizing, arming, and disciplining them, and for governing such part of them as may be employed in the service of the United States, reserving to the states respectively the appointment of the officers, and the authority of training the militia according to the discipline prescribed by Congress.

189. The object of this power is to secure uniformity in the organization and discipline of the militia, and, as a consequence, efficiency in case of actual service. By an Act passed in 1820, Congress provided that the system of discipline and field exercise, which is observed by the regular army, should also be observed by the militia.

Seat of Government.

190. Congress exercise exclusive legislation, in all cases whatever, over such district (not exceeding ten miles square) as may, by cession of particular states, and the acceptance of Congress, become the seat of the government of the United States; and they also exercise like authority over all places purchased by the consent of the legislature of the state in which the same shall be, for the erection of forts, magazines, arsenals, dockyards, and other needful buildings.

191. The seat of government in the first instance was New York. It was then removed to Philadelphia, and, finally, in 1800, to Washington, a district of ten miles square, called the District of Columbia, having been ceded to the United States by Maryland and Virginia. Having exclusive jurisdiction within the District, Congress possess the means of protecting themselves from insult or interruption, without dependence on the state authorities, who might, in particular exigencies, be unable or unwilling to defend them.

192. As the District of Columbia is not a state in the sense of the Constitution, the citizens cannot send Representatives to Congress, nor vote for President or Vice-President of the United States. Recently [1871], however, a territorial government was established for them, with the right to a delegate in Congress.

Jurisdiction over Forts, &c.

193. If a place is purchased in any state, *with the consent of its legislature*, for the erection of a fort, magazine, arsenal, dockyard, or other needful buildings, then Congress possesses exclusive jurisdiction over such place, and neither civil nor criminal process, issued under the authority of the state, can be executed therein, unless the state expressly reserves

that privilege. Moreover, the inhabitants of such place cease to be inhabitants of the state, and cannot exercise any civil or political rights under the laws of the state.

194. On the other hand, if a purchase of territory is made by the United States in any state for public purposes, *without the consent of its legislature*, then the jurisdiction of the state over such territory remains full and complete. It has not the right, however, to tax such territory.

General Power of Congress.

195. Had the Constitution made no provision to that effect, it would have been implied that Congress might employ the means necessary to execute the powers with which they were invested. But it has not been left to implication: the Constitution expressly authorizes Congress to make all laws which shall be *necessary* and *proper* for carrying into execution the foregoing powers, and all other powers vested by the Constitution in the government of the United States, or in any department or officer thereof.

196. Congress has no power under this clause of the Constitution, except to provide the means of executing the powers vested in the government of the United States, or in any department or officer thereof. If the means be appropriate to this end, if they are not prohibited, and are consistent with the

letter and spirit of the Constitution, then they are authorized.

Concurrent powers of Legislation in the States.

197. It is important to observe that the powers which the Constitution confides to Congress are not necessarily exclusive. It is only in cases where the Constitution, in express terms, grants an exclusive authority to Congress, or the nature of the authority requires that it should be exclusively exercised by Congress, that the subject is taken from the state legislatures.

198. It is believed that there are only three cases where the authority of Congress is exclusive: First, when it is made exclusive in express terms; secondly, when a power is confided to Congress, and the states are prohibited from exercising a like power; thirdly, when a power is granted to Congress to which a similar power in the states would be absolutely and totally contradictory and repugnant.

199. In all other cases the states retain concurrent authority with Congress, subject, however, to two limitations. One is, that if the state legislation conflicts with that of Congress, then it is void, because the laws of the United States made in pursuance of the Constitution are supreme. The other is, that where, from the nature of the power, its exercise *at*

the same time by both Congress and the states would be inconsistent, then the legislation of Congress, in pursuance of that power, absolutely suspends the legislative power of the states over the same subject. Thus, Congress are authorized to establish uniform laws on the subject of bankruptcy, but the states may pass bankrupt laws, provided there be no act of Congress in force establishing a uniform law on that subject. In this instance, it is not the mere existence of the power, but its exercise, which is incompatible with the exercise of the same power by the states. When Congress passes a uniform law, the partial laws of the states must yield to it.

POWERS DENIED TO CONGRESS.

200. We have seen in the preceding pages what Congress may do. The next step leads us to consider what they may not do.

The Slave Trade.

201. In the first place, the migration or importation of such persons as any of the states existing at the time of the adoption of the Constitution should think proper to admit, were not to be prohibited by the Congress prior to the year one thousand eight hundred and eight; but a tax or duty might be imposed on such importation not exceeding ten dollars for each person.

202. The object of this clause was to prevent Congress from interdicting the slave trade prior to the year 1808. At the time the Constitution was framed, there was a strong feeling in several of the states in favor of that trade, and in deference to that feeling Congress were inhibited to abolish it prior to the year above named. Congress, however, at an early day prohibited American citizens from carrying on the traffic between foreign countries; and they

passed a prospective Act in 1807, prohibiting the importation of slaves into the United States after January 1, 1808. As the penalties of this Act were not sufficient to put an end to the traffic, another Act was passed in 1820, declaring the slave trade piracy, and punishing those engaged in it with death.

Habeas Corpus.

203. The privilege of the writ of *habeas corpus* cannot be suspended, unless when, in cases of rebellion or invasion, the public safety may require it.

204. The words *habeas corpus* mean "that you have the body," and the writ, so called, is directed to the person charged with illegally detaining another in custody, commanding him to produce the body of the prisoner, and make known the cause of his detention. If no sufficient ground of detention appears the party is entitled to an immediate discharge. The courts of the United States issue the writ of *habeas corpus* in cases falling within their jurisdiction, and the state courts possess a like authority in cases falling within theirs; so that a prompt and efficacious remedy and a convenient tribunal are provided for every case of illegal restraint of a man's liberty.

204½. Under the judiciary act of 1789, the justices of the Supreme Court, as well as the district judges, have power to grant writs of *habeas corpus* for the purpose of inquiry into the cause of commitment; provided, however, that such writs shall not extend to prisoners in jail, unless they are in custody under or by color of the authority of the United States, or are committed to trial before some court of the same, or unless it is necessary to bring them into court to testify. It will be observed, therefore, that by the terms of this act, no judge of a United States court can issue a *habeas corpus* to extend to a prisoner in custody under sentence or execution of a state court, no matter whether the imprisonment is under civil or criminal process, except for the single purpose of using such prisoner as a witness. By subsequent acts, however, the power of the justices of the supreme and district courts was extended to cases of a prisoner or prisoners in jail or confinement, committed or confined by any authority, for any act done or omitted to be done, in pursuance of a law of the United States, or any order, process, or decree of any judge or court thereof; and to cases where subjects or citizens of a foreign state, and domiciled therein, are committed, or confined, or are in custody, under or by any authority, or law, or process founded therein, of the United States, or of any one of them, for or on account of any act done or omitted under any alleged right, title, authority, privilege, protection, or exemption, set up or claimed under the commission, or order, or sanction of any foreign state or sovereignty, the validity or effect whereof depends upon the law of nations, or under color thereof; and, lastly, to cases where any person is restrained of liberty in violation of the Constitution, or of any treaty or law of the United States.

$204\frac{3}{4}$. It is only in the foregoing cases that the Federal judiciary has jurisdiction of this writ; in all other cases arising under the specific laws of the several states or under the common law, the party aggrieved must seek his remedy in the appropriate state court. But the state tribunals have no right, through the writ of *habeas corpus,* to inquire into the lawfulness of restraint under the authority of the United States; they may indeed issue the writ when illegal restraint upon liberty is alleged, yet when it is served upon the Federal officer, having the prisoner in charge, and his return shows that he is held under Federal authority, the state court can proceed no further with the case. Such officer is not bound to obey the state process, except so far as to make known to the state tribunal the authority under which the prisoner is held.

205. In cases of rebellion or invasion, the public safety may require that the government should have the power to imprison dangerous persons on grounds that might not be sufficient to prevent their discharge should they or others for them apply to the courts for a writ of *habeas corpus.* In such cases, therefore, Congress may suspend the privilege of the writ;

the judicial interpretation of this clause of the Constitution being that the President has not the power to suspend the privilege of the writ, and that it can only be done by Congress. The power of the President is limited to executing the laws; he has no power to suspend them. The latter, so far as it exists, is a legislative function, and by the Constitution belongs to Congress. We may add, that a suspension of the privilege of the writ, does not suspend the writ itself; the writ issues as a matter of course: on its return the court decides whether the applicant is entitled to proceed further

Attainder.

206. No bill of attainder or *ex post facto* law shall be passed.

207. The English Parliament possess the power of inflicting death upon a person, and confiscating his property by a special act, without allowing him an opportunity to defend himself before a judicial tribunal. Such special act is called a bill of attainder. In passing it Parliament may disregard the rules of evidence and the principles of justice, and condemn a man to death from mere political rancor, hatred, or suspicion. In favorable times such a power is not likely to be exercised; in bad times it is sure to be abused. Congress are, therefore, prohibited from passing a bill of attainder.

Ex Post Facto Laws.

208. By an *ex post facto* law is meant a law that makes an act done before the passing of the law, and which was innocent when done, criminal; or which aggravates a crime, and makes it greater than when it was committed; or which changes the punishment, and inflicts a greater punishment than the law annexed to the crime when committed; or which alters the legal rules of evidence, and receives less or different testimony than the law required at the time of the commission of the offence, in order to convict the offender; or subjects an individual to a pecuniary penalty for an act which, when done, involved no responsibility, or if it deprives him of any valuable right — such as the right to follow a lawful calling — for acts not punishable when committed, or not punishable in that mode, the law will be *ex post facto* and void.

209. *Ex post facto* laws relate to penal and criminal proceedings, which impose penalties or forfeitures, and not to civil proceedings, which affect private rights retrospectively. And a law that *mitigates* the character or punishment of a crime already committed, does not fall within the prohibition of the Constitution, such law being in favor of the citizen, and mollifying, in his behalf, the rigor of the criminal law.

Capitation Tax.

210. We have elsewhere seen that no capitation or other direct tax can be laid, unless in proportion to the census or enumeration which the Constitution directs to be taken (sec. 135 *et seq.*), and it is unnecessary, therefore, to recur to the subject again.

Taxes on Exports prohibited.

211. No tax or duty can be laid on articles exported from any state, and this for the obvious reason that such a tax would bear unequally. If a tax, for instance, could be laid on all tobacco exported, then the states producing and exporting tobacco would bear exclusively a portion of the public burthen which ought to be divided among all the states. By imposing a heavy tax upon any single article of export, the states not exporting such article might remain exempt from contributing their just share of the public taxes. Indeed, if Congress were not altogether prohibited from laying taxes on exports, they might derive the whole revenue of the government from the exports of particular states. Hence the propriety of the prohibition.

No Preference to be given to the Ports of one State over those of another.

212. No preference can be given, by any regulation of commerce or revenue, to the ports of one state over those of another; nor can vessels bound to or from one state, be obliged to enter, clear, or pay duties in another.

213. The object of this clause is to prevent advantages being granted to one state at the expense of others; and also to prevent that system of commercial regulation by which, before the Revolution, vessels sailing from the colonies for Europe were compelled to proceed first to Great Britain, and sail from some British port. The power thus to interrupt voyages for the benefit of particular states is properly denied to Congress.

Appropriations.

214. No money can be drawn from the Treasury, but in consequence of appropriations made by law; and a regular statement and account of the receipts and expenditures of all public money must be published from time to time.

215. Two checks are here provided against an improper use of the public money. In the first place,

before money can be drawn from the Treasury by the President or any officer of the government, a specific appropriation must be made by Congress. In the second place, a statement of the receipts and expenditures of all public money must be published from time to time, and Congress are thus made responsible to the people for any extravagance in the public expenditures. Not even the creditors of the government can be paid out of the Treasury, without Congress first making an appropriation for that purpose. Their only remedy is an application to Congress, as they can neither sue the United States nor have a lien on the public property which may happen to be in their possession. But now, by the act of Feb. 24, 1855, claims against the United States, and counter claims, are determined by a court of claims, from whose decision, in certain cases, an appeal lies to the Supreme Court.

Titles of Nobility, &c.

216. No title of nobility can be granted by the United States; and no person holding any office of profit or trust under them can, without the consent of Congress, accept of any present, emolument, office, or title, of any kind whatever, from any king, prince, or foreign state.

217. Titles of nobility are incompatible with that

spirit of equality which pervades our system of government, and the United States are, therefore, prohibited to grant them. The states, likewise, in their individual character, as we shall see hereafter, are equally prohibited to grant any title of nobility.

218. Officers of the United States are forbidden to accept, without the consent of Congress, any present, emolument, office, or title, of any kind whatever, from any king, prince, or foreign state, lest foreign governments should in that manner unduly influence our affairs. When presents are sent to the President, as they sometimes are from foreign princes, they are usually deposited in the public offices—it not being thought courteous to decline them.

POWERS DENIED TO THE STATES.

219. Having now considered the restrictions which the Constitution imposes upon Congress, we next proceed to consider the restrictions which are imposed upon the states.

Prohibition as to Treaties, &c.

220. The first is, that no state shall enter into any treaty, alliance, or confederation; grant letters of marque and reprisal; coin money; emit bills of credit; make anything but gold and silver coin a tender in payment of debts; pass any bill of attainder, *ex post facto* law, or law impairing the obligation of contracts, or grant any title of nobility.

221. It will be observed that several of these restrictions are among the number of those which we have already enumerated as being imposed on Congress: such, for example, as the prohibition to pass any bill of attainder, *ex post facto* law, or to confer any title of nobility. But for the most part, the powers which are here denied to the states may be exercised by Congress.

222. It is obvious that if the states were at liberty to make treaties, or form alliances and confederations, there would be no harmony or uniformity in our relations abroad, and no stability or independence at home. The separate states might form conflicting treaties and alliances, and enter into such engagements as would give foreign powers an opportunity to interfere and exercise a control in our affairs. The treaty-making power, therefore, is denied to the states, and confided to the government of the Union.

Letters of Marque and Reprisal.

223. Though letters of marque and reprisal are sometimes granted in peace, as a means of redress, and not as a measure of hostility, yet they are usually the precursor of war whether so intended or not. Hence it would be most unwise to put it in the power of a single state to involve the whole country in hostilities, by adopting a measure which would be likely to incur them.

Coinage.

224. The power to coin money is denied to the states, and confided exclusively to Congress, in order to secure a uniform currency in place of coins of various forms and weights, which otherwise might be put in circulation. It has been said, and truly, that

if the states could coin money and regulate its value, then there might be as many different currencies as states. Yet the same practical consequence follows from the power which the states exercise of authorizing the circulation of bank paper as currency. A uniform *metallic* currency is secured by giving to Congress the exclusive authority to coin money and regulate its value; but there is no such uniformity in the paper currency of the states, which is the actual and well-nigh universal substitute for coin. The paper currency of the states, however, under recent legislation, has almost entirely given way to the circulation of the national banks. It has been supposed that the taxing power of Congress was confined to the purpose of raising revenue; yet in aid of the circulation of the national banks, the state banks have well-nigh been taxed out of existence, and this too under acts of Congress passed avowedly for the purpose. The constitutionality of this taxation too has been sustained by the Supreme Court of the United States. The force of the decision, however, is much impaired by the fact that it was the decision of a divided court.

Bills of Credit.

225. Bills of credit, which the states are prohibited to emit, are bills issued by a state on the faith of the state, and intended to circulate through the commu-

nity in the ordinary business of life as money. Bonds or obligations, therefore, issued by or on behalf of a state, binding it to pay money at a future day, for purchases which it has made, or for services received, or for money borrowed, are not bills of credit within the meaning of the Constitution. Neither are the bills issued by banks which a state incorporates, though the state may be a stockholder in such banks, or even the exclusive owner of the stock. But if the bills were issued on the credit of the state, instead of the credit of the funds of the bank, it would be otherwise.

Legal Tender.

226. Though the states authorize the issue of paper money, they are prohibited to make anything but gold and silver coin a tender in payment of debts. During the Revolutionary War and subsequently, attempts were frequently made to maintain the credit of paper money, by making it a tender in payment of debts—the result being gross wrong and injustice to creditors. Instances were not wanting where the debtor had received gold and silver, and yet was enabled to pay his debt with paper money, which was so depreciated as to be nearly worthless. It was to prevent the possibility of such grievances that the states were inhibited to make anything but gold and silver coin a tender in payment of debts.

Bills of Attainder and Ex Post Facto Laws.

227. We have already seen that Congress can pass no bill of attainder or *ex post facto* law (sec. 206), and for the same reason the states are equally prohibited to pass such laws. A power to do so could scarcely be exercised by the most judicious hands without oppression and injustice, and is, therefore, denied both to Congress and the state legislatures. But an *ex post facto* law, it will be recollected, relates to criminal proceedings. Hence the Constitution does not prohibit the states from passing retrospective laws which relate to civil proceedings, though such laws may destroy vested interests or affect private rights. A contract, for example, founded upon an illegal or immoral consideration is void; yet it would not be repugnant to the Constitution for a state to enact that all such contracts should be valid and binding upon the parties, though such enactment would be retrospective in its character.

Impairing the Obligation of Contracts.

228. The states can pass no law impairing the obligation of contracts; but there is nothing in the Constitution that forbids Congress from passing such

laws. Any deviation from the terms of a contract, by which the intentions of the parties are enlarged or abridged, or in any manner changed, as by postponing or accelerating the period of performance, imposing conditions not expressed in the contract, or dispensing with those which are expressed, however minute or apparently immaterial in their effect upon the contract, impair its obligation. Laws, however, which merely affect or change the remedy by which a contract is enforced, do not impair its obligation, provided effectual though different means of enforcing it remain.

229. The contracts to which the Constitution refers are those which respect property, or some object of value, and confer rights which may be asserted in a court of justice. Such contracts, whether entered into between individuals, or states, or corporations, or between a state and individuals, cannot be impaired by state legislation.

230. A state is as much inhibited from impairing its own contracts, or contracts to which it is a party, as it is from impairing the obligation of contracts between individuals. When, therefore, a state makes a grant of lands or corporate powers, an implied contract arises that it will not reassert the right with which it has parted. Thus, when a state makes a conveyance of land, such conveyance cannot be re-

scinded or revoked by the state. The right of the state is extinguished by the grant, and cannot be resumed. But it may discontinue offices created by statute, or take away the compensation without abolishing the office; or, as we shall see in the next section, abolish or change the organization of municipal corporations at any time, unless forbidden by its own fundamental law. It cannot, however, take from a municipal corporation the power to levy taxes to pay existing debts; nor authorize stay of execution in a case where the debtor has expressly waived it; nor deprive persons of the right to maintain suits because participating in or sympathizing with rebellion against the United States; nor invalidate a contract for the purchase or hire of slaves, such contract being valid when made; nor compel a public creditor to surrender his securities, and accept others bearing a less interest.

231. With regard to charters, they are divided into two classes, namely, public and private charters. The former are such as relate to public purposes alone, to charters that incorporate towns, cities, &c. Such charters merely grant political power, and are not contracts within the meaning of the Constitution, and may, therefore, be changed or modified at the pleasure of the state legislatures—care being taken, of course, not to violate or infringe private rights. But private charters, such as are granted to banks, colleges, insurance or turnpike companies, are con-

tracts between the state and the corporators, and cannot, therefore, without the consent of such corporators, be altered or repealed by the state, unless the right to do so has been expressly reserved; nor can the state subject a private corporation to forfeiture of its franchises for that which was not a cause of forfeiture originally; nor repeal a statute which made the stockholders liable for its debts contracted while it was in force.

232. On the other hand, where a state grants rights to private corporators in matters in which the public interest is concerned, no implied contract arises that it will not make a similar grant to other corporators, though the second grant may operate to the injury of the first. Thus, where a state granted a charter to a company authorizing them to build a bridge, and take tolls thereon for a certain period, it was held that it might equally grant a similar charter to another company, though the second bridge should be on the same line of travel as the first, and accommodate the same passengers, and thus be the means of diverting its tolls; and this for the reason that as no direct engagement was made that no other bridge should be built, no such engagement was to be implied; because in such cases no rights are to be taken from the public and given to corporations by implication.

232½. The state under the right of eminent domain, to which all contracts are subject, may appropriate corporate franchises, as well as every other species of property. If suitable provision is made by the legislature for the compensation of those whose property or franchise is injured or taken away, under this paramount power, there is no violation of public faith or private right. On the contrary, the obligation of the contract created by the charter is thereby recognized.

233. A state law which discharges a debtor from his obligation to pay a debt which was contracted *before* the passage of the law, is unconstitutional and void, because it not only impairs, but destroys the obligation of the contract. But a law which operates upon and discharges *future* contracts is constitutional, provided such contracts are made within the state, and between citizens of the state. And this for the reason that parties to a contract have reference to the existing laws of the place where it is made. They know that these laws act upon their contract and govern its construction, validity, and obligation. A state, too, may prescribe the remedies to enforce contracts, and pass statutes of limitation, as well as change the rules of evidence, applicable to existing causes of action or to pending suits. And it may too abolish existing remedies, provided other and efficient ones are substituted or remain, and may increase ex-

emptions of property from execution arising out of existing contracts.

233½. A statute making the bills of a bank, whereof the state owns the stock, receivable in payment of all debts due the state, constitutes a contract between the state and those who receive the bills; and the state is thereby precluded from depriving the bill holders of the rights acquired under such statute, by repealing it. So too a state, upon a consideration therefor, may agree to exempt property from taxation, or to exempt it beyond a certain rate or amount, and such exemption cannot be revoked. On the other hand, if the exemption is a mere privilege, it may be revoked at any time, in the legislative discretion.

Prohibition as to Imposts, &c.

234. No state can, without the consent of Congress, lay any imposts or duties on imports or exports, except what may be absolutely necessary for executing its inspection laws; and the net produce of all duties and imposts, laid by any state on imports or exports, are for the use of the Treasury of the United States; and all such laws are subject to the revision and control of Congress.

235. While the states possess a concurrent power of taxation with the United States, there is one source of revenue which they cannot touch without the consent of Congress; that is, they cannot lay

any imposts or duties on imports or exports, except what may be absolutely necessary for executing their inspection laws. By this prohibition on the states to impose duties, and confiding the power to Congress alone, a uniform system of duties is secured, and rival systems on the part of the several states prevented.

236. For the purpose, however, of executing their inspection laws, the states may impose such duties on imports or exports as may be absolutely necessary; but the money arising therefrom is not for the use of the state. The net produce must be paid into the Treasury of the United States, and the laws imposing such duties are subject to the revision and control of Congress. Inspection laws are such as require certain commodities specified in the laws themselves, and whether produced at home or imported from abroad, to be examined, and their quality approved before they are exported or offered for domestic use.

237. A state law requiring the importer of goods, by wholesale, bale, or package, to take out a license and pay for it, under certain penalties or forfeitures for neglect or refusal, has been held by the Supreme Court to be unconstitutional and void, both because it interferes with the power of Congress to regulate commerce, and violates the prohibition which we are now considering, that no state can lay a duty on imports.

238. The Court regarded a tax on the sale of an article imported only for sale, or a tax on the thing imported, in the hands of the importer, as equivalent to a tax or duty upon imports. If such a tax could be imposed at all, it might be made so heavy as to amount to a prohibition, and thus defeat the revenue by import, so far as it is drawn from importations into the state laying the tax.

239. But when the importer has so acted upon the thing imported that it has become incorporated and mixed up with the mass of property in the country, it loses its distinctive character as an import, and becomes subject to the taxing power of the state.

Tonnage Duties, &c.

240. No state can, without the consent of Congress, lay any duty of tonnage, keep troops or ships of war in time of peace, enter into any agreement or compact with another state, or with a foreign power, or engage in war unless actually invaded, or in such imminent danger as will not admit of delay.

241. By tonnage is meant the capacity or burden of a vessel expressed in tons, which is ascertained by measurement, according to a rule prescribed by an Act of Congress; and the duty, so called, is the sum levied upon such vessel after a certain rate for every ton. The states are prohibited to impose such a duty,

or any duty on a ship, without the consent of Congress, for the same general reason that they are prohibited to impose duties on imports or exports without a similar consent, namely, that there may be a uniform system in all the states: in a word, that harmony may prevail in place of diversity, inequality, and discord.

Troops and Ships of War.

242. The states are prohibited to keep troops or ships of war in time of peace, without the consent of Congress, because the power to declare war, raise and support armies, and to provide and maintain a navy, is confided to Congress, and is supposed to be adequate to the security of the states without their keeping up military armaments themselves. Besides, if the states were at liberty to keep on foot standing forces, it might lead to collisions among them or with the general government, or end in the establishment of military governments in place of civil institutions.

Compacts.

243. The restriction, that no state shall enter into any agreement or compact with another state, or with a foreign power, without the consent of Congress, is intended to prevent any infringement of the rights of the national government. The words are used in their broadest sense, and were intended to

cut off all negotiation and intercourse between the state authorities and foreign nations. They cannot, for example, without the consent of Congress, enter into any agreement or compact, express or implied, to deliver up fugitives from justice from a foreign state, who may be found within their limits.

244. Coupled with the previous clause, which prohibits any state from entering into any treaty, alliance, or confederation, the door is closed against any political or other arrangements and combinations, on the part of the states, which might interfere with the stability and harmony of the Union, or the rights and controlling authority of the government of the Union. The consent of Congress, however, to agreements between states need not be express, but may be implied from its legislation on the subject.

Prohibition as to War.

245. The power of declaring war being confided to Congress, it is very proper that the states should be prohibited to engage in it without the consent of Congress, unless actually invaded, or in such imminent danger as will not admit of delay. Otherwise all the states might become involved in war in consequence of the folly, caprice, or rashness of any single state. When actually invaded, or in such imminent danger as will not admit of delay, the

states have the right to raise troops without the consent of Congress, and provide for their own safety.

Implied Prohibition as to Taxation.

246. In addition to the express prohibitions upon the states, which we have mentioned in the preceding sections, there is an important implied one, namely, that the states shall not tax any of the instruments employed by the government in the execution of its powers. They cannot tax the mail, nor the mint, nor patent rights, nor the papers of the custom-house, nor judicial process, nor stock issued for loans to the United States, nor the salaries of officers of the United States, nor ships, nor munitions of war, nor, in a word, any of the means or agencies employed to carry into effect the objects of the government.

THE PRESIDENT.

General Observations.

247. The vigor and efficiency of every government essentially depend upon its executive authority. Hence all lawgivers have bestowed great attention upon its constitution. If too much power is confided to this department, it may be employed to overthrow the other departments, and concentrate all the powers of government in its own hands; if too little, then its action is languid, and imbecility marks all its movements. Various expedients have been resorted to in order to guard against abuse on the one hand, and weakness on the other. In some cases the executive power has been divided among several persons; in others concentrated in a single hand. In some cases it has been declared hereditary; in others elective, while again there has been no distinct executive department—all the powers of government being united in a single assembly. This was the case under the Confederation, the whole power of the government being vested in Congress.

248. The evils of this latter system had been too

clearly demonstrated to admit of any division of opinion in the Convention, as to the necessity of separating the executive from the legislative and judicial departments, and giving it a distinct sphere. The general sentiment too was in favor of confiding it to the hands of a single officer, though there were voices who advocated a plural executive. It was said that an executive composed of three persons, chosen from the three great divisions of the country, would prevent any one division from prejudicing the interests of the other divisions. But the dissensions and factious consequences which had always arisen in governments where the executive authority was divided among several persons, were sufficient to restrain the Convention from repeating that error.

Unity of the Executive.

249. The nature of man and the lessons of history conspired to show the importance of unity in the executive department of the government. Hence the executive power was vested in a President of the United States of America. He holds his office during the term of four years, and, together with the Vice-President, chosen for the same term, is elected in the mode described in a succeeding section.

Term of Office.

250. Though the President is re-eligible for successive terms, yet, in practice, he never has been a candidate for a third election. It was the opinion of many enlightened statesmen that he should be elected for seven years, and be ineligible afterwards. "But the practice adopted," says Mr. Jefferson, "I think is better, allowing his continuance for eight years, with a liability to be dropped at half way of the term, making that a period of probation."

251. Doubtless the frequent election of an executive magistrate for a great country is attended with evils; it creates great excitement, involves much expense and loss of time on the part of the electors, and renders the policy of the government in a measure uncertain. But, on the other hand, were he to hold office for life or a long term of years, the struggle to obtain possession of so splendid a prize might break out in dissensions, tumults, and civil war. Besides, such an executive would not have that sense of dependence on the public approbation which is an essential check on his conduct.

Mode of Election.

252. Each state appoints, in such manner as the legislature thereof may direct, a number of electors

equal to the whole number of Senators and Representatives to which the state may be entitled in the Congress; but no Senator or Representative, or person holding an office of trust or profit under the United States, can be appointed an elector.

253. The legislature of each state may directly choose the electors itself, or refer the choice to the people. All the state legislatures, it is believed, have adopted the latter course, which is thought to be preferable to the former, as giving less opportunity for corrupt combinations or coalitions.

254. That the electors may be impartial persons, and unbiassed by their connection with or dependence on the President in office, who might desire a re-election, it is provided that no member of Congress, nor any person holding an office of trust or profit under the United States, shall be an elector. Each state has the same number of electors as Senators and Representatives, which gives to the several states in the choice of President the same relative weight that they possess in Congress.

255. When chosen, the electors meet in their respective states and vote by ballot for President and Vice-President, one of whom, at least, must not be an inhabitant of the same state with themselves. They must name in their ballots the person voted for as President, and, in distinct ballots, the person

voted for as Vice-President, and they must make distinct lists of all persons voted for as President, and of all persons voted for as Vice-President, and of the number of votes for each, which lists they must sign and certify, and transmit sealed to the seat of the government of the United States, directed to the President of the Senate. The President of the Senate is required, in presence of the Senate and House of Representatives, to open all the certificates, and the votes must then be counted. The person having the greatest number of votes for President is President, if such number be a majority of the whole number of electors appointed; and if no person have such majority, then from the persons having the highest numbers, not exceeding three, on the list of those voted for as President, the House of Representatives must choose immediately, by ballot, the President. But, in choosing the President, the votes must be taken by states, the representation from each state having one vote. A quorum for this purpose consists of a member or members from two-thirds of the states, and a majority of all the states are necessary to a choice. And if the House of Representatives do not choose a President whenever the right of choice devolves upon them, before the fourth day of March next following, then the Vice-President acts as President, as in the case of the death or other constitutional disability of the President. The person having the greatest number of votes as Vice-President is Vice-President, if such number be a majority of the whole number of electors appointed, and if no person have a majority, then from the two highest numbers on the list, the Senate must choose the Vice-President; a quorum for the purpose consists of two-thirds of the whole number of Senators, and a majority of the whole number is necessary to a choice. But no person constitutionally ineligible to the office of President is eligible to that of Vice-President of the United States.*

* The present mode, as described in the text, of electing the President and Vice-President, is different from the mode originally provided by the Constitution. But, in the year 1804, the Constitution was amended, and the amendment superseded the original clause. It may be useful, however, for reference and comparison to insert the original provision in this place. It is as follows:

The electors shall meet in their respective states, and vote by ballot for two persons, of whom one at least shall not be an inhabitant of the same state with themselves. And they shall make a list of all the persons voted for, and of the number of votes for each; which list they shall sign and certify, and transmit sealed to the seat of the government of the United States, directed to the President of the Senate. The President of the Senate shall, in the presence of the Senate and House of Representatives, open all the certificates, and the votes shall then be counted. The person having the greatest number of votes shall be the President, if such number be a majority of the whole number of electors appointed; and if there be more than one who have such a majority, and have an equal number of votes, then the House of Representatives shall immediately choose by ballot one of them

Time of Election.

255. Congress may determine the time of choosing the electors, and the day on which they shall give their votes; which day shall be the same throughout the United States.

256. By an Act of Congress, passed in 1845, the electors are required to be chosen in each state on the Tuesday next after the first Monday in November. By a previous Act, passed March 1, 1792, the electors are directed to meet in their respective states, at a place appointed by the legislature thereof, on the first Wednesday in December in every fourth year succeeding the last election, and vote by ballot for President and Vice-President. They are then to make and sign their certificates of all the votes by them given, and to seal up the same, certifying on each that a list of the votes of such state for President and Vice-President is contained therein; and

for President; and if no person have a majority, then, from the five highest on the list, the said House shall in like manner choose the President. But in choosing the President, the votes shall be taken by states; the representation from each state having one vote; a quorum for this purpose shall consist of a member or members from two-thirds of the states, and a majority of all the states shall be necessary to a choice. In every case, after the choice of the President, the person having the greatest number of votes of the electors shall be Vice-President. But if there should remain two or more who have equal votes, the Senate shall choose from them by ballot the Vice-President.

appoint a person to take charge of and deliver one of the certificates to the President of the Senate, at the seat of government, before the first Wednesday of the next ensuing January; another of the certificates is to be forwarded forthwith by the Post-office to the President of the Senate at the seat of government; and the third is to be delivered to the judge of the district in which the electors assembled.

257. The President of the Senate, on the second Wednesday in February succeeding every meeting of the electors, in the presence of both Houses of Congress, opens all the certificates, and the votes are then counted and the result declared. It will be observed that the Constitution does not determine how questions which may arise as to the regularity and authenticity of the returns of the electoral votes, or the right of the persons who gave the votes, or the manner or circumstances in which they ought to be counted, shall be decided. In the absence of any rule as to the jurisdiction or mode of proceeding in such cases, a partisan majority in Congress, as has been justly remarked, may always have the power to defeat the will of the people in the count, or to precipitate civil war. It is provided by law, that the term of four years, for which a President and Vice-President shall be chosen, shall, in all cases, commence on the fourth day of March next succeeding the day on which the votes of the electors shall have been given.

Qualifications for President.

258. No person, except a natural born citizen, or a citizen of the United States at the time of the adoption of the Constitution, is eligible to the office of President; neither is any person eligible to that office who has not attained to the age of thirty-five years, and been fourteen years a resident within the United States.

259. Were foreigners or naturalized citizens eligible to the office of President, foreign powers might have an opportunity to intermeddle in our affairs. They might aid by money or other influences in elevating to the Presidency men of foreign birth and predilections, and the interests of the country be thus put in jeopardy. The exception in favor of such persons of foreign birth as were citizens of the United States at the time of the adoption of the Constitution, is now practically extinct. The distinguished patriots who had so faithfully served their adopted country during the revolutionary struggle, and out of respect and gratitude to whom this exception was introduced into the Constitution, have all passed away. No one, therefore, but a natural born citizen can now be elected to the office of President.

260. In respect to the qualification of age, it will be observed that the Constitution has established a gradation, as it were, in the legislative and executive

departments. A Representative must be twenty-five, a Senator thirty, and the President thirty-five. Without adverting to the relative importance of the duties confided to each, and which may require a higher qualification, in point of age, in the case of the President than is required in the case of a Representative or Senator, it may be remarked that it will rarely happen that the people of all the states will have had an opportunity to become familiar with the character, capacity, and principles of a citizen of any one state before he has attained the age of thirty-five; or that he will have acquired that experience, knowledge, gravity of character, and solidity of judgment that ought to distinguish a President of the United States.

261. By fixing the qualification, too, at thirty-five, an opportunity is afforded for previous service in both branches of Congress, where the future candidate may acquire experience in public affairs, and at the same time become known to his countrymen. By requiring, also, a previous residence of fourteen years within the United States, he will be likely to have formed habits of attachment to his country and devotion to its institutions. The residence contemplated by the Constitution, however, does not exclude persons who are temporarily abroad in the public service, or on their private affairs.

Disability of the President.

262. In case of the removal of the President from office, or of his death, resignation, or inability to discharge the powers and duties of the office, the same devolves on the Vice-President, and the Congress may by law provide for the case of removal, death, resignation, or inability, both of the President and Vice-President, declaring what officer shall then act as President, and such officer shall act accordingly, until the disability be removed or a President be elected.

263. In pursuance of the constitutional provision, Congress have provided that in case of the removal, death, resignation, or inability of the President and Vice-President, the President of the Senate *pro tempore*, and in case there shall be no President of the Senate, then the Speaker of the House of Representatives, for the time being, shall act as President, until the disability be removed or a President shall be elected.

264. When the Vice-President succeeds to the office of President, upon the removal, death, or resignation of the latter, he discharges its duties until the close of the term for which the President was elected. But when he succeeds to the office upon the inability of the President, he discharges its powers and duties

only so long as such inability continues. On the other hand, when the offices of President and Vice-President both become vacant, Congress have provided that a new election shall take place. Meanwhile the President of the Senate *pro tempore*, or, if there be no President of the Senate, then the Speaker of the House of Representatives, acts as President.

265. Congress have also provided that the only evidence of a refusal to accept, or of a resignation of the office of President or Vice-President shall be an instrument in writing declaring the same, and subscribed by the person refusing to accept or resigning, as the case may be, and delivered into the office of the Secretary of State.

266. In order to provide for the exigency of a vacancy in the office of President during the recess of Congress, it has become usual, as we have already seen (sec. 76), for the Vice-President, a few days before the termination of each session of Congress, to vacate the chair of the Senate, to enable that body to elect a President *pro tempore.*

His Salary.

267. The Constitution declares that the President shall, at stated times, receive for his services a compensation which shall neither be increased nor diminished during the period for which he shall have

been elected, and he shall not receive within that period any other emolument from the United States, or any of them.

268. In the first term of Washington's administration the salary of the President was fixed at the sum of twenty-five thousand dollars *per annum.* This sum, together with the use of the Presidential mansion and furniture, was deemed adequate to the becoming support of the President. No change was ever made in respect thereto, until March third, eighteen hundred and seventy-three, when Congress enacted that on and after the fourth day of March ensuing, the President should receive in full, for his services during the term for which he had been elected, the sum of fifty thousand dollars *per annum,* payable monthly. By the same act, the salary of the Vice-President was increased from eight to ten thousand dollars *per annum.*

269. A salary should be granted the President, otherwise persons of moderate fortunes might be deterred from accepting the office, however well qualified in other respects to perform its duties; or, on the other hand, be impeded in their performance by pecuniary difficulties, and exposed to unworthy temptations in consequence of them. Congress should not have the power to increase or diminish this salary during the period for which the President was elected, because his independence would be thus endangered or destroyed. In order to prevent a diminution of

his salary on the one hand, or to obtain its augmentation on the other, he would be apt to take the will of Congress for his guide, instead of performing his duties in a firm, impartial manner. It has been justly remarked that a control over a man's living is, in most cases, a control over his actions.

His Oath.

270. Before entering upon the execution of his office, the President is required to take the following oath:—"I do solemnly swear (or affirm) that I will faithfully execute the office of President of the United States; and will, to the best of my ability, preserve, protect, and defend the Constitution of the United States."

His Powers.

271. The President is Commander-in-Chief of the Army and Navy of the United States, and of the militia of the several states, when called into the actual service of the United States; he may require the opinion, in writing, of the principal officer in each of the executive departments upon any subject relating to the duties of their respective offices; and he has power to grant reprieves and pardons for offences against the United States, except in cases of impeachment.

Commander-in-Chief of the Army.

272. Experience has demonstrated that the success of military and naval operations essentially depend upon the vigor, promptitude, and energy with which they are executed, and that these qualities are most likely to be displayed where the command is intrusted to a single person. Hence the propriety of confiding the command of the public force to the President. When the legislative authority has declared war, the President, to whom its execution is confided, is bound to carry it into effect. He has a discretion vested in him as to the manner and extent; but he cannot lawfully transcend the rules of warfare established among civilized nations.

273. The President is not obliged, in person, to take the command of the army, but he may delegate his right to another officer; nor is he obliged to command, in person, the militia when they are called into the public service, but may confer the chief command upon another. In his capacity of commander-in-chief of the army and navy, he may establish rules and regulations for their government; and the rules and orders emanating from the War and Navy Departments are to be considered as emanating from him.

Executive Departments.

274. To enable the President to perform the various important duties devolving on him, Congress have at different times created executive departments, to which are allotted functions peculiar to each. These departments are now six in number, and are designated as follows:—First, Department of State; secondly, Department of the Navy; thirdly, Department of War; fourthly, Department of Treasury; fifthly, Post-Office Department; sixthly, Department of the Interior.

275. These departments are aids and instruments by which the executive authority of the government is administered. The chief officer of each is termed Secretary, and the name of the department over which he presides at once suggests the character of the duties confided to him.

276. Thus the Secretary of State, in subordination to the President, has the general charge of all matters relating to our foreign affairs; the Secretary of War, of all matters relating to the control and disposition of the army, the erection of fortifications, and the purchase of arms and munitions; the Secretary of the Navy, of all similar matters relating to the naval establishment of the United States; the Secretary of the Treasury has charge of the finances of the

government, and is required, at the commencement of every session, to lay before Congress a report on the subject of finance, containing estimates of the public revenue and public expenditures, and plans for increasing the revenue; and the Secretary of the Interior, which is a new department created in 1849, has supervision of the patent, land, pension, and census offices; and also of Indian affairs, mines, and the public buildings.

277. The Postmaster-General, as we have elsewhere remarked, has charge of the postal affairs of the country; and the law officer of the government, termed the Attorney-General, is bound to prosecute and conduct all suits in which the United States are a party, and to give his advice and opinion, when required by the President, or when requested by the heads of any of the departments, touching any matters that may concern their departments.

278. The Secretaries, the Postmaster-General, and Attorney-General, are appointed by the President, with the advice and consent of the Senate, and by recent legislation, are only removable with the like advice and consent. He may require their opinion in writing upon any subject relating to the duties of their respective offices; but in practice he assembles them as a cabinet council. Hence they are spoken of as the Cabinet. It was not until within a comparatively recent period that the Post-

master-General was regarded as one of the Cabinet, and summoned to take part in its deliberations.

279. Though the President may require the written opinion of his Cabinet, as above mentioned, he has no such authority with respect to the judiciary. The judges can only be called upon to decide controversies brought before them in legal form, and are bound to abstain from extra-judicial opinions upon questions of law.

Reprieves and Pardons.

280. The President has power to grant reprieves and pardons for offences against the United States, except in cases of impeachment.

281. A reprieve is a suspension of the punishment awarded to an offence for a designated time; a pardon is a total remission of such punishment, and may be granted before as well as after trial and conviction. The President has also power to order a *nolle prosequi* in any stage of a criminal proceeding in the name of the United States. He may pardon too either absolutely or conditionally, provided the condition be compatible with the genius of the Constitution and laws. The power to pardon is not limited to any particular grade of offence; but, with one or two exceptions, which we shall presently notice, extends to all, and includes the remission of fines, penalties, and forfeitures. And as it is confirmed by

the Constitution, Congress can impose no limitations or restrictions upon its exercise.

282. The prominent exception to the President's power of pardoning is in cases of impeachment, and he is restrained in those cases lest he should screen from punishment his favorites or dependants, who might be convicted of political or official offences. It is thought too that he would not have the power to pardon a person sentenced for a contempt of either branch of Congress, though it is admitted that he may pardon for a contempt of court.

Treaty Power.

283. The President has also the power, by and with the advice and consent of the Senate, to make treaties, provided two-thirds of the Senators present concur.

284. Under this power the President, with the sanction of the Senate, may make treaties of peace, commerce, alliance, and of every other description, subject to only one limitation, namely, that the treaties thus made shall not violate the principles of the Constitution. For example, the Constitution provides that no title of nobility shall be granted by the United States. If, therefore, the President should negotiate a treaty, one of the stipulations of which provided that the United States should grant titles of nobility, such stipulation would be absolutely void.

285. In England the power to make treaties is vested in the king. His authority in this respect is absolute—the treaties he makes not being subject to the revision and ratification of either house of Parliament. In the ancient republics, this power was usually lodged in the legislative branch of the government. At Athens and Rome, for example, the assemblies of the people made the determinations respecting peace and war.

286. The Constitution of the United States combines the advantages of both systems. By making the President the organ of communication with foreign powers, and the agent in the negotiation of treaties, secrecy and despatch are secured, which are essential in order to profit by new and unexpected information, or new and unexpected changes in the fortune of affairs. On the other hand, by making the validity of his negotiations depend upon the consent of two-thirds of the Senators present, a guard is provided against an abuse of the trust thus confided to him.

287. When a treaty has been adjusted under the direction of the President, it is laid before the Senate for ratification. They deliberate upon it in what is termed *executive* session, that is, in secret, with closed doors. They may wholly reject it, or ratify a part of its stipulations, rejecting others, or recommend additional articles. If alterations are made, both the

President and the foreign government must assent to them before the treaty becomes effective and binding. And even where no alterations are proposed by the Senate, and they ratify a treaty in full, the President may still withhold his assent to it. The Constitution does not determine, when treaties and acts of Congress are in conflict, which shall prevail; but judicially, it is held that a treaty may supersede a prior act of Congress, and an act of Congress may supersede a prior treaty.

Nominations to Office.

288. The President nominates, and, by and with the advice and consent of the Senate, appoints ambassadors, other public ministers, and consuls, judges of the Supreme Court, and all other officers of the United States whose appointments are not otherwise provided for in the Constitution, and which shall be established by law; but Congress may, by law, vest the appointment of such inferior officers as they think proper in the President alone, in the courts of law, or in the heads of departments.

289. The President possesses the power to negotiate treaties, and, with obvious propriety, appoints the ministers through whom the negotiations are carried on. He may appoint diplomatic agents of any rank, at any place, and at any time in his discretion,

and this power, it seems, cannot be limited by Congress. He is also charged with the execution of the laws, and with equal propriety appoints the officers who are to aid him in the performance of his duty. But this power of appointment cannot be exercised without the advice and consent of the Senate, except in the case of inferior officers, whose appointments Congress may, by law, vest solely in the President, or in the courts of law, or in the heads of departments.

290. Knowing, therefore, that the character and fitness of the persons whom he may select for office are to be scrutinized by the Senate, he will naturally be more cautious in making the selection. And if, from misinformation or error, he nominates unsuitable persons, the Senate can save the public from the consequences likely to follow a bad appointment, by rejecting the nomination. The constitutional agency of the Senate in appointments to office, however, is solely confined to a simple affirmation or rejection of the President's nominations; they cannot originate an appointment.

291. After the President has nominated, and the Senate confirmed his nomination, he may still withhold the appointment from the nominee. The appointment is not final and complete until the President has signed the commission. It has been thought even that it was not complete until *delivery* of the

commission; but the Supreme Court have held otherwise.

Removals from Office.

292. The power of the President to appoint to office, with the advice and consent of the Senate, was early in the history of the government construed to mean that he might remove, at his pleasure, all officers appointed and commissioned by him, unless the Constitution itself had fixed their tenure of office. The Constitution, for example, provides that the judges of the courts of the United States shall hold their offices during good behavior. These the President cannot remove; but most of the officers appointed by him, according to the long established doctrine and practice, whether civil or military, were removable at his pleasure. But Congress, by the act of fifth April, eighteen hundred and sixty-nine, has provided that civil officers, appointed by and with the advice and consent of the Senate, shall not be removed, unless with the like advice and consent.

Power to Fill Vacancies.

293. The President has power to fill up vacancies that may happen during the recess of the Senate, by granting commissions which expire at the end of their next session.

294. As vacancies are continually occurring in the

public service from death, resignation, or expiration of office, the President is empowered to fill such vacancies. Were it otherwise it would be necessary, in order to provide for the appointment of officers, to keep the Senate in perpetual session, or summon them together at great expense and inconvenience whenever a vacancy should occur.

295. The appointments thus made in the recess of the Senate, expire at the end of their next session. If, when the Senate assembles, the President should, with their concurrence, appoint the same person he had appointed in the recess, this would be a new appointment, and not a continuation of the old one. So that the bond for the faithful discharge of duties under the first appointment, would not be applicable to acts done under the second.

296. If the Senate, on the other hand, should not approve the nomination of an officer who had been appointed in the recess, his commission is not thereby determined, but continues in force until the end of the session, unless sooner determined by the President. By recent legislation, Congress has declared that if no appointment, by and with the advice and consent of the Senate during its next session, be made to an office which had become vacant and been filled during the recess of the Senate, then such office shall remain in abeyance, without any salary, fees, or emoluments attached thereto, until such time as it is filled with the advice and consent of the Senate.

297. Again, if an office should be created by law while the Senate is in session, and the President should neglect to make any nomination to it, he could not, without special authority, appoint to such office after the adjournment of the Senate, because the vacancy does not happen during the recess.

His Communications to Congress.

298. The President must, from time to time, give to the Congress information of the state of the Union, and recommend to their consideration such measures as he shall judge necessary and expedient.

299. In obedience to this injunction of the Constitution, the President, annually, at the opening of each session of Congress, addresses a written message to them containing information respecting the foreign and domestic affairs of the country, together with such recommendation of measures as he may deem necessary and proper. He also sends them special messages on other occasions whenever he deems it necessary. President Washington and President Adams were in the habit of meeting both Houses in person, at the opening of each session of Congress, and delivering a speech to them; but upon the accession of Mr. Jefferson to the Presidency the practice was discontinued and written messages substituted.

His Power to Convene Congress, &c.

300. The President may, on extraordinary occasions, convene both Houses, or either of them, and in case of disagreement between them, with respect to the time of adjournment, he may adjourn them to such time as he shall think proper.

301. The propriety of this power speaks for itself. Unexpected exigencies constantly occur in the affairs of nations which demand immediate action, and when this action should require the co-operation of Congress, the public interest might suffer serious detriment if that co-operation could not be obtained in advance of the regular session.

302. Of nearly equal necessity as the power to convene Congress on extraordinary occasions, is the power to adjourn them in cases of disagreement. When they cannot agree as to the time of adjournment, the interposition of the President at once puts an end to the controversy, and thus prevents distraction in the public councils.

Receives Ambassadors.

303. The President receives ambassadors and other public ministers; that is, they present their credentials to him, and receive his official recognition of

their character. Until this be done they cannot enter upon the performance of their duties. The President is the representative of his country in all diplomatic negotiations, and naturally is intrusted with the power to appoint and receive the agents through whom such negotiations are carried on. It will be observed, however, that he appoints with the concurrence of the Senate (sec. 288, &c.), but receives without their participation. The reason of this difference is, probably, to be found in the fact, that it would be attended with too much inconvenience to summon the Senate together whenever a foreign minister should be sent hither, in order that he might be received and enter upon the discharge of his duties.

304. The President may, in his discretion, refuse to receive a foreign minister; but if his refusal should be for inadequate cause, and unaccompanied with proper explanations, it might bring on hostilities. He may refuse to receive him upon the ground of his former bad character, or former offensive conduct, or because the special subject of the embassy is not proper or not convenient for discussion; or because the state from which he is sent may be divided and distracted by civil wars, so as to render it inexpedient to acknowledge the supremacy of either party.

305. The President may also, when the language

or conduct of a foreign minister is inadmissible, suspend his functions by a refusal to treat with him, or make application to his sovereign for his recall, or dismiss him and require him to depart within a reasonable time. It is said, too, that where the safety of the state absolutely requires it, force may be applied to confine or send him away.

306. This, however, is all that can be done. A foreign minister may insult the government to which he is deputed, or violate its laws, and he cannot be made amenable either to its civil or criminal jurisdiction. By the law of nations, from which the privileges of foreign ministers derive their origin and support, he is exempted from all allegiance, and from all responsibility to the laws of the country to which he is sent; and this immunity extends to the attendants attached to his person.

307. To give effect to this principle of the law of nations, Congress, by an Act passed in 1790, declared that all writs and process issued out of any court of the United States, or of a particular state, or by any judge or justice, whereby any ambassador or other public minister of any foreign prince or state, or any servant of any such ambassador or minister, might be arrested, or his goods and chattels be seized, should be deemed utterly void.

308. Public ministers are divided into four classes:

First, ambassadors and papal legates or nuncios; second, envoys, ministers, or others accredited to sovereigns; third, ministers resident accredited to sovereigns; fourth, *chargés d'affaires* accredited to the minister of foreign affairs. Ambassadors are considered as peculiarly representing the sovereign or state by whom they are delegated, and entitled to the same honors to which their constituent would be entitled, were he personally present. The right of sending ambassadors is exclusively confined to crowned heads, the great republics, and other states entitled to royal honors. So far, however, as the nature of their respective functions is concerned, there is no essential difference between public ministers of the first and second class. The United States have always appointed ministers of the second class.

309. Though the President is expressly empowered to *appoint* consuls, he is not expressly empowered to *receive* them. He has, however, always exercised the power, it being deemed an incident of his authority; and foreign consuls have never been allowed to act as such without his *exequatur*, or written declaration authorizing them to perform the duties of their office.

310. A consul is a commercial agent, and not a public minister in the sense of the law of nations. He is not, therefore, entitled to the immunities which that law confers upon such ministers. Both in civil

and criminal cases he is subject to the laws of the country in which he resides, equally with all other persons. If guilty too of illegal or improper conduct, his *exequatur* may be revoked, which puts an end to his functions.

Executes the Laws.

311. It is the duty of the President to take care that the laws are faithfully executed.

312. The very nature of the executive office would seem to imply that the President should perform this function of executing the laws. But it is expressly enjoined on him by the Constitution, and he may employ the forces of the United States in performing it. Accordingly, when combinations exist among the citizens of one or more of the states to obstruct or defeat the execution of acts of Congress, and hostilities thence arise, and assume the dimensions of war, it is the duty of the President to prosecute opposing hostilities, offensive as well as defensive, and upon a scale to suit the exigencies of the occasion. And he cannot, in the exercise of his powers, be restrained by injunction, from carrying into effect an act of Congress, upon an allegation that such act is unconstitutional. Nor can he be arrested, imprisoned, or detained, while discharging the duties of his office; in all civil cases, his person possesses an official inviolability.

Commissions Officers.

313. It is also the duty of the President to commission all the officers of the United States.

314. A commission is the official certificate or written evidence of an appointment to office. It is signed by the President, and if a civil commission, it is made the duty of the Secretary of State to affix to it the seal of the United States.

May be impeached.

315. We have seen elsewhere (sec. 78) that the President, Vice-President, and all civil officers of the United States are to be removed from office on impeachment for, and conviction of, treason, bribery, or other high crimes and misdemeanors. It is unnecessary, therefore, to recur to the subject again.

316. We have thus concluded our survey of the office of President; and we shall now proceed to investigate the powers and duties of the judicial department of the government.

THE JUDICIAL POWER OF THE UNITED STATES.

In whom vested.

317. The judicial power of the United States is vested in one Supreme Court, and in such inferior courts as Congress may, from time to time, ordain and establish.

318. The object of the Constitution was to constitute three great departments of government: the legislative, the executive, and the judicial department. The first is to pass laws, the second to approve and execute them, and the third to expound and enforce them.

The Supreme Court.

319. The Supreme Court was instituted by the Constitution itself; but its organization was left to Congress. As at present organized, it consists of a Chief Justice and eight Associate Justices, any six of whom make a quorum, and it holds one term annually, at the seat of government, and such adjourned or special terms as it may find necessary for the despatch of business, commencing, formerly, on the first Monday of December; but now on the second Monday

of October of each year. The salary of the Chief Justice is ten thousand five hundred dollars *per annum,* that of the Associate Justices ten thousand dollars *per annum.*

320. The importance of a supreme tribunal, in which may meet and terminate appeals from inferior judicatures, is very obvious. Uniformity of decision is thus secured, and the inferior courts kept within the limits of their jurisdiction.

Inferior Courts.

321. While the Constitution imperatively requires that there shall be *one* Supreme Court, it is left to Congress to determine the number of inferior courts which they will establish. They are bound to create some inferior courts, because the Constitution contemplates cases of which only such courts can, in the first instance, take cognisance; but whether one or more, Congress must, in their discretion, decide.

Circuit Courts.

322. In the exercise of this discretion, Congress have established Circuit and District Courts. Circuit Courts are established in each of the nine great circuits into which the United States are divided. Each circuit is composed of a certain number of districts; the states of Rhode Island, Massachusetts, New Hampshire, and Maine, for example, being districts, and together constituting the first circuit.

323. In each of these districts there are annually held two Circuit Courts, which consist of a judge of the Supreme Court, a judge of the Circuit Court, and a judge of the District Court. The judge of the Supreme Court, however, is not obliged to attend more than one term of the Circuit Court in any district of his circuit during any period of two years. The circuit judge resides in his circuit, and possesses the same power and jurisdiction therein as the justice of the Supreme Court allotted to the circuit. The powers of the justices of the Supreme Court, as judges of the Circuit Court, are unaffected by the act (April 10, 1869) creating the circuit judges, except that the latter have the appointment of the clerks of said court.

Jurisdiction of the Circuit Courts.

324. The jurisdiction of the federal courts depends exclusively on the Constitution and laws of the United

States. And as Congress have the power to establish inferior courts, they have, as a necessary consequence, the right to define their respective jurisdictions. Congress, accordingly, have vested the Circuit Courts with original jurisdiction, concurrently with the courts of the several states, of all suits of a civil nature, where the matter in dispute exceeds five hundred dollars, exclusive of costs, and the United States are plaintiffs, or an alien is a party, or the suit is between a citizen of the state where the suit is brought, and a citizen of another state. They have, too, original jurisdiction of all suits arising under any law of the United States relative to copyrights, and the rights growing out of inventions and discoveries.

325. They have also exclusive jurisdiction of all crimes and offences against the United States, the punishment of which is capital, and concurrent jurisdiction with the District Courts of all such crimes and offences where the punishment is not capital. And they have appellate jurisdiction from all final decrees and judgments in the District Courts, where the matter in dispute, exclusive of costs, exceeds fifty dollars.

Jurisdiction — Original — Exclusive — Concurrent—Appellate.

326. By original jurisdiction is meant the right vested in a court to hear and determine a cause in the first instance. This may be an exclusive or concurrent right. It is exclusive when the particular cause can only be brought before the particular court; and concurrent when it may be brought in any one of two or more courts. By appellate jurisdiction is meant the right vested in a court to hear and determine appeals from the judgment of another court. The Circuit Courts, it will be observed, exercise jurisdiction of each description, that is, exclusive, concurrent, and appellate.

District Courts.

327. The United States are at present divided into forty-five districts, in each of which is established a District Court. These districts, for the most part, consist of an entire state, though in several of the states it has been found necessary to constitute two or more districts. A District Court is composed of a single judge, who holds annually four stated terms, and also special courts, in his discretion. In districts where the business of the court may require it to be done for the purposes of justice, the judges

must hold monthly adjournments of the regular terms for the trial of criminal causes.

Jurisdiction of the District Courts.

328. The District Courts have concurrent jurisdiction with the Circuit Courts of all crimes and offences against the United States, the punishment of which is not capital. They have also exclusive, original cognisance of all civil causes of admiralty and maritime jurisdiction; of all seizures under the impost, navigation, or trade laws of the United States, where the seizures are made upon the high seas, or on waters within their districts navigable from the sea with vessels of ten or more tons burthen; and of all other seizures made under the laws of the United States, and also of all suits for penalties and forfeitures incurred under those laws.

329. They have also cognisance, concurrent with the Circuit and state courts, of causes where an alien sues for a tort committed in violation of the law of nations, or of a treaty of the United States; and concurrently with the Circuit Courts, and the courts and magistrates of the several states, of all suits at common law where the United States, or any officer thereof, acting under the authority of an Act of Congress, shall sue. They have also jurisdiction, exclusively of the state courts, of all suits against

consuls, vice-consuls, except for offences of a capital nature.

Clerks.

330. The Supreme, Circuit, and District Courts have power to appoint clerks; and this power of appointment includes that of removal. These clerks have the custody of the seal and records, and are bound to sign and seal all process, and seasonably to record the decrees, judgments, and determinations of their respective courts. In addition to an oath of office, they are required to give security in the sum of two thousand dollars, for the faithful discharge of their duties.

Marshals.

331. The President and Senate appoint a Marshal for each judicial district, whose duty it is to attend the District and Circuit Courts when sitting therein, and to execute, within the district, all lawful precepts which are directed to him, and issued under the authority of the United States. He may command all necessary assistance in the execution of his duty, and may appoint one or more deputies, who are removable at his pleasure, as well as at the pleasure of the District or Circuit Courts. The Marshal himself is appointed for the term of four years; but at the same time, with the concurrence of the Senate, is re-

movable at the pleasure of the President. Before entering upon the duties of his office, he is obliged to give security in the sum of twenty thousand dollars for the faithful performance of the same by himself and his deputies, and, together with his deputies, to take an oath of office.

Tenure of Office.

332. The judges both of the Supreme and inferior Courts hold their offices during good behavior, and at stated times receive for their services a compensation which cannot be diminished during their continuance in office.

333. The President, with the advice and consent of the Senate, appoints the judges of the Supreme and inferior Courts; but he does not possess the power of removing them. Their tenure of office is independent of both government and people; it depends absolutely upon themselves. Their continuance in office is during good behavior. If they behave properly they are secured in their places for life; if they misbehave, if they violate the trust confided to them, they may be impeached, and, if convicted, removed from office.

Their Salary.

334. The Constitution has also secured to the judges a fixed provision for their support. They

receive at stated times for their services a compensation which cannot be diminished during their continuance in office. Owing to the fluctuations in the value of money and in the state of society, it may happen that the salaries given to the judges at one time will be inadequate at another. Congress may, therefore, increase them; but they have no power to diminish them. Nor can a tax be imposed upon the salary of a judge. Hence the judges can never be deterred from their duty by the apprehension of being placed in a less eligible situation.

Extent of the Judicial Power.

335. The judicial power extends to all cases, in law and equity, arising under the Constitution, the laws of the United States, and treaties made, or which shall be made under their authority; to all cases affecting ambassadors, other public ministers, and consuls; to all cases of admiralty and maritime jurisdiction; to controversies to which the United States are a party; to controversies between two or more states; to controversies between a state, when plaintiff, and citizens of another state; to controversies between citizens of different states, and between citizens of the same state claiming lands under grants of different states, and between a state, or the citizens thereof, and foreign states, citizens, or subjects.

Meaning of Case.

336. A *case*, in the sense of the Constitution, is a controversy between parties which has taken a shape for judicial decision. *Cases in law* mean cases in which relief is sought according to the principles and practice of the common law; *cases in equity* mean cases in which relief is sought according to the principles and practice of equity jurisprudence. A case is said to *arise* under the Constitution, or a law, or a treaty of the United States, when its correct decision depends upon the construction of either.

The several Descriptions of Cases.

337. It will be observed that the Constitution extends the judicial power to eleven descriptions of cases:

First, To all cases arising under the Constitution.

Second, To all cases arising under the laws of the United States.

Third, To all cases arising under treaties made by their authority.

Fourth, To all cases affecting ambassadors or other public ministers, and consuls.

Fifth, To all cases of admiralty and maritime jurisdiction. Admiralty and maritime jurisdiction relates to acts or injuries done upon the high sea, or within the ebb and flow of the tide, or upon the navigable lakes and rivers of the United States; and to contracts, claims, and services appertaining to commerce and navigation. In civil suits of admiralty and maritime jurisdiction the proceedings are conducted according to the course of the civil law, and without a jury. Congress may, however, give to either party the right of trial by jury, or make such other change in the mode of proceeding as it deems proper.

338. Sixth, To controversies to which the United States shall be a party. The United States may sue, but they cannot be sued.

Seventh, To controversies between two or more states.

Eighth, To controversies between a state, when plaintiff, and citizens of another state, or foreign citizens and subjects. As the Constitution originally stood, a state might be sued by a citizen of another state. But the states deemed this derogatory to their dignity, and the Constitution was therefore amended, so that the states may sue; but cannot be sued by individuals, whether they be citizens of another state, or citizens or subjects of any foreign state.

Ninth, To controversies between citizens of different states. Citizenship, when spoken of in the Constitution, in reference to the jurisdiction of the courts of the United States, means nothing more than residence. But it has been held by the Supreme Court that a free negro of the African race, whose ancestors were brought to this country and sold as slaves, is not a citizen within the meaning of the Constitution, nor entitled to sue in that character in the federal courts.

Tenth, To controversies between citizens of the same state claiming lands under grants of different states.

Eleventh, To controversies between a state or the citizens thereof and foreign states, citizens, or subjects. A foreign state cannot be sued; she can only appear in the federal courts as plaintiff.

Original Jurisdiction of the Supreme Court.

339. In all cases affecting ambassadors, other public ministers, and consuls, and those in which a state shall be a party, the Supreme Court has *original* jurisdiction.

340. The original jurisdiction of the Supreme Court is founded entirely on the character of the parties: the nature of the controversy is not contemplated by the Constitution. And this jurisdiction Congress have no power to extend; but whether it is both original and exclusive, or may be exercised by the subordinate federal courts, has never been authoritatively determined. The Act of Congress, however, organizing the Supreme Court, does not regard it as

exclusive. On the contrary, it declares, for example, that in all suits or proceedings *against* ambassadors, or other public ministers or their domestics, or domestic servants, the jurisdiction shall be exclusive; but *not* exclusive when the suit is brought *by* an ambassador or other public minister, or where a consul or vice-consul is a party.

Appellate Jurisdiction.

341. In all the other cases before mentioned (sec. 335), the Supreme Court has appellate jurisdiction, both as to law and fact, with such exceptions and under such regulations as Congress may make.

342. Of the eleven descriptions of cases to which the judicial power extends, the Supreme Court, it will be observed, has original jurisdiction of but two, namely, cases affecting ambassadors, other public ministers, and consuls; and cases in which a state shall be a party. The other nine it can only decide by way of appellate jurisdiction; that is, they must, in the first instance, be brought in a lower court, and the judgment of such lower court may then be re-examined and reversed, or affirmed in the Supreme Court.

343. The rule established by Congress, under their power to make exceptions and regulations respecting the appellate jurisdiction of the Supreme Court, pro-

vides that the Circuit Courts may re-examine, reverse, or affirm the final decrees and judgments of the District Courts in civil actions when the matter in dispute exceeds fifty dollars, exclusive of costs; and that the Supreme Court may re-examine, reverse, or affirm the final judgments and decrees of the Circuit Courts when the matter in dispute exceeds, exclusive of costs, two thousand dollars.

Appeals from the State Courts.

344. The appellate jurisdiction of the Supreme Court is not limited to the inferior courts of the United States. It is the *case*, and not the *court*, that gives the jurisdiction. It extends, therefore, to the state courts as well as to the subordinate courts of the United States. Congress have accordingly provided that a final judgment or decree, in any suit in the highest court of law or equity of a state, may be re-examined and reversed or affirmed in the Supreme Court in three descriptions of cases:—First, When the validity of a treaty, or statute of, or authority exercised under the United States is drawn in question, and the decision is against its validity. Secondly, When the validity of a statute of, or an authority exercised under any state is drawn in question on the ground of their being repugnant to the Constitution, treaties, or laws of the United States,

and the decision is in favor of their validity. Thirdly, When the construction of any clause of the Constitution, or of a treaty, or statute of, or commission held under the United States, is drawn in question and the decision is against the title, right, privilege, or exemption specially claimed under the authority of the United States.

Territorial Courts.

345. Having now reviewed the provisions of the Constitution which relate to the judicial power, we have only to add, in concluding this branch of our subject, that the Courts established by Congress for the territories are not among the courts in which is vested any part of such judicial power. They are legislative courts, created in virtue of the sovereignty which exists in the government over its territories; and the jurisdiction with which they are invested is not a part of the judicial power which the Constitution contemplates. Hence Congress may limit the tenure of office of the judges, and make such provision with regard to their salaries as they deem proper. And, as the President may remove all officers appointed and commissioned by him, when the Constitution has not otherwise provided, he may with the advice and consent of the Senate, remove a territorial judge.

TRIALS AND IMMUNITIES.

Trial by Jury in Criminal Cases.

346. The trial of all crimes, except in cases of impeachment, must be by jury; and such trial must be held in the state where the crimes were committed. But, when not committed within any state, the trial must be at such place or places as the Congress may by law have directed.

347. A jury is a body of men, selected according to a prescribed mode, to try questions of fact in civil and criminal suits, and who are under oath or solemn affirmation to decide the facts truly and faithfully, according to the evidence laid before them. Juries of this kind are called *petit* (or small) juries; but there is another kind of jury, called a grand jury, whose duties are of a different character, as we shall presently see. A *petit* jury consists of twelve men; a grand jury of not less than twelve, nor more than twenty-three, and twelve at least must concur in every accusation.

348. One of the articles of *Magna Charta* declares that no man shall be arrested, nor imprisoned, nor banished, nor deprived of life, &c., but by the judgment of his peers, that is, the judgment of a jury, or by the law of the land. This right of trial by

jury was very dear to our ancestors, who brought it with them to America. It prevailed in all the colonies anterior to the Revolution, and was secured by a special provision in all their constitutions when they became independent states. The Constitution of the United States also requires that the trial of all crimes, except in cases of impeachment, shall be by jury; and, that the accused party may not be subjected to unnecessary expense and difficulty in procuring testimony, the trial must be held in the state where the crime was committed.

349. But when crimes are committed upon the high seas, or elsewhere, out of the limits of any state, then the trial must be at such place as Congress may by law have directed. Congress accordingly have directed that the trial, in such cases, shall take place in the district where the offender is apprehended, or into which he may be first brought.

Immunities secured to Accused Persons.

350. In addition to the original provision of the Constitution respecting trial by jury, there are several amendatory provisions which were designed still further to protect the rights of individuals, and to guard against injustice and wrong. These provisions are found among the amendments to the Constitution, but their consideration seems naturally to belong to this place. The first is as follows:—

351. No person shall be held to answer for a capital, or otherwise infamous crime, unless on a presentment or indictment of a grand jury, except in cases arising in the land or naval forces, or in the militia, when in actual service, in time of war, or public danger; nor shall any person be subject, for the same offence, to be twice put in jeopardy of life or limb; nor shall be compelled, in any criminal case, to be a witness against himself; nor be deprived of life, liberty, or property, without due process of law; nor shall private property be taken for public use without just compensation.

Grand Juries.

352. Grand juries are summoned to attend the Circuit and District Courts, whenever a judge of either shall so direct. They are not necessarily summoned at every term, because their services may not be needed. Their duty is to make inquiry and present all offences within the jurisdiction of the court they are summoned to attend. They sit in secret and examine the testimony *against* the accused party, which is laid before them by the prosecuting officer of the government.

353. If they do not think it sufficient to support the charge which is set forth in the bill of indictment, that is, in the written accusation, they endorse on

the back of the bill the words 'not a true bill,' or 'not found,' or 'ignoramus,' which means, We know nothing of it. The accused is then entitled, if in custody, to be discharged. An innocent party is thus spared the pain and obloquy of being publicly tried upon a criminal charge.

354. On the other hand, if the grand jury think the evidence is sufficient to support the indictment, they endorse on the back of it, 'a true bill.' It is then said to be found, and is publicly taken into court by the jury; the accused is then held to answer, and may be put on his trial.

355. It will be observed that the intervention of a grand jury is imperatively required only when the crime is capital, that is, punishable with death, or otherwise infamous. In crimes of an inferior grade their services may be dispensed with, and an accused party be tried without their first having found a bill of indictment against him. But, in practice, all crimes of whatever grade are laid before them, and only tried upon indictments found by them.

Courts-martial.

356. In the government of the army and navy, and also of the militia when in actual service, in time of war, or public danger, offences are tried and punished by courts-martial, according to the rules

established by Congress. A court-martial is composed of military or naval officers, for the trial of offences against the laws of the service in the army or navy.

No Person to be put twice in Jeopardy.

357. No person shall be subject for the same offence to be twice put in jeopardy of life and limb; that is, he shall not be again tried for such offence, after having been once acquitted or convicted. The court, however, may discharge a jury from giving a verdict without the consent of the prisoner whenever, in their opinion, there is a manifest necessity for doing so, or the ends of public justice would be otherwise defeated. In such case he may be tried again, because it is not considered that he has been put in jeopardy of life and limb. He may also be tried again when, after a verdict of conviction, the court grants a new trial in his favor. In neither case is he judicially considered to have been put in jeopardy.

Not to be a Witness against himself.

358. No person shall be compelled in any criminal case to be a witness against himself. This is to prevent any resort to those cruel and unjust means which have been employed in other countries to extort a confession of guilt. An accused party is presumed

to be innocent until his guilt is made to appear by legal proof. His own voluntary confession may be given in evidence; but he cannot be *compelled* to testify against himself.

Not to be deprived of Life unless, &c.

359. No person shall be deprived of life, liberty, or property, without due process of law, that is, without legal warrant therefor being first obtained in the regular course of legal proceedings.

Private Property not to be taken for Public Use unless, &c.

360. Private property cannot be taken for public use without just compensation. A similar provision is to be found in the constitutions of the several states, so that neither the government of the United States nor that of the individual states can arbitrarily take private property. It must be taken only for the public use, and just compensation must be made for it.

Rights of Defendants in Criminal Cases.

361. Another of the amendatory articles declares that, in all criminal prosecutions, the accused shall enjoy the right to a speedy and public trial, by an

impartial jury of the state and district wherein the crime shall have been committed, which district shall have been previously ascertained by law, and be informed of the nature and cause of the accusation; be confronted with the witnesses against him; have compulsory process for obtaining witnesses in his favor; and have the assistance of counsel for his defence.

362. We have seen in a previous section (sec. 346) that the trial of all crimes must be by jury, and also be held in the state where they were committed; but this amendment of the Constitution was intended still further to insure justice to a person accused of a criminal offence. It secures to him a *speedy* and *public* trial by an impartial jury of the state and district wherein the crime was committed, which district must have been previously ascertained by law.

363. He is to be informed of the nature and cause of his accusation. This is done in the indictment, which carefully sets forth both; and Congress have provided that in cases of treason the accused shall have a copy of the indictment delivered to him three entire days at least before the trial, and in other capital cases at least two entire days before the trial.

364. He is to be confronted with the witnesses against him, that is, they must give in their testimony in his presence. He is also to have compulsory pro-

cess for obtaining witnesses in his favor, and to have the assistance of counsel for his defence.

Excessive Bail not to be required.

365. One of the amendments to the Constitution declares that excessive bail shall not be required, nor excessive fines imposed, nor cruel and unusual punishments inflicted.

366. Bail is the security given for the release of a prisoner, and his appearance in court at a designated time to meet his trial. By Act of Congress bail must be admitted upon all arrests in criminal cases, except where the punishment may be death, in which case it shall not be admitted but by the Supreme or a Circuit Court, or by a justice of the Supreme Court, or a judge of a District Court, who must exercise their discretion whether to admit it or not, upon a consideration of the nature and circumstances of the offence, and of the evidence and usages of law. It would be vain, however, to provide for the discharge of persons in custody upon their giving bail, if such provision could be defeated by the courts requiring excessive bail. They might not be disposed to require it; but the Constitution has very properly put it out of their power to exercise any discretion in the matter.

Trial by Jury in Civil Cases.

367. We have now seen that the Constitution provides that the trial of all crimes, except in cases of impeachment, shall be by jury; and we have considered the various securities that have been devised to prevent wrong and injustice in criminal prosecutions. But it was made a great objection to the Constitution that there was no express provision for a trial by jury in civil cases. Besides, it was said that as the Supreme Court had appellate jurisdiction *both as to law and fact*, they would have the power practically to review and overturn the verdicts of juries, and thus destroy the benefits of that mode of trial.

368. To meet these objections the Constitution was amended, and it was expressly provided that in suits at common law, when the value in controversy should exceed twenty dollars, the right of trial by jury should be preserved; and no fact, tried by a jury, should be otherwise re-examined in any court of the United States than according to the rules of the common law.

369. The common law here meant is the common law of England. This law has been incorporated, so far as it is applicable to their situation, into the jurisprudence of all the states, except the state of

Louisiana, where the civil law prevails. And by suits at common law is meant all suits, not of equity or admiralty jurisdiction, in which legal rights are determined according to the principles of the common law, no matter what may be the peculiar form of the suit. And in all suits of this character, where the value in controversy exceeds twenty dollars, the trial must be by jury, unless the parties to the suit waive the benefit of such trial.

370. According to the common law, facts once tried by a jury are never re-examined, unless a new trial be granted by the court before which the suit is depending; or unless the judgment of such court be reversed, by a superior tribunal, for some error of law in its proceedings, and a new trial be granted in consequence. It is therefore only in these two modes that a fact, once tried by a jury, can again be re-examined in any court of the United States.

TREASON.

In what it Consists.

371. To prevent subordinate acts from being construed as treason, which, in former times, was frequently done in England, the Constitution declares that treason against the United States shall consist only in levying war against them, or in adhering to their enemies, giving them aid and comfort.

372. Levying war is the assembling of a body of men, in a condition to make war, for the purpose of overthrowing the government, or resisting its powers. A conspiracy or agreement to levy war does not amount to treason. There must be an actual assembling of men, with the intention and capacity to levy war, to constitute a levying of war, or, in other words, treason. But if war be actually levied, all those who perform any part, however minute, or owever remote from the scene of action, and who are really leagued in the general attempt, are to be considered traitors.

373. Treason against the United States may also consist in adhering to their enemies, giving them aid and comfort. Delivering up prisoners and deserters to the enemy is treason within this clause. And so

it has been held is the carrying of provisions towards the enemy with intent to supply him, though that intention should be defeated.

How many Witnesses necessary in cases of Treason.

374. No person shall be convicted of treason unless on the testimony of two witnesses to the same overt act, or on confession *in open court.*

Punishment of Treason.

375. Congress have power to declare the punishment of treason, but no attainder of treason shall work corruption of blood or forfeiture, except during the life of the person attainted.

376. The common law prescribes the following mode of punishment for the crime of treason: 1. That the offender be drawn to the gallows, and not be carried or walk, though usually (by connivance, at length ripened into law) a sledge or hurdle is allowed, to preserve the offender from the extreme torment of being dragged on the ground or pavement. 2. That he be hanged by the neck, and cut down alive. 3. That his entrails be taken out and burned while he is yet alive. 4. That his head be cut off. 5. That his body be divided into four parts. 6. That his head and quarters be at the king's disposal.

377. Such a barbarous and cruel mode of punishment could only have been devised in an uncivilized and ferocious age. It is a source of just pride and congratulation, that a spirit of mildness and humanity characterizes all the provisions of the Constitution of the United States that relate to crimes and punishments. In a previous section we have seen that it is expressly provided that excessive fines shall not be imposed, nor cruel and unusual punishments inflicted. So that, although Congress may declare the punishment of treason, such punishment must not be cruel or unusual. The punishment actually declared by Congress is death by hanging.

378. Another restraint upon the power of Congress to declare the punishment of treason is, that no attainder of treason shall work corruption of blood or forfeiture, except during the life of the person attainted.

379. By attainder of treason is meant that stain or corruption of blood which, by the common law, follows upon conviction of treason. A person thus attainted forfeits all his lands, and tenements, and goods, and can neither inherit an estate from his ancestors, nor transmit one to his posterity. To prevent this unjust punishment of the innocent descendants of a man convicted of treason, the Constitution provides that no attainder of treason shall

work corruption of blood or forfeiture, except during the life of the person attainted. And Congress by law have declared that no conviction or judgment, for any capital or other offences, shall work corruption of blood or any forfeiture of estate.

INTERSTATE PRIVILEGES AND REGULATIONS.

State Records, etc.

380. Full faith and credit must be given in each state to the public acts, records, and judicial proceedings of every other state. And Congress may, by general laws, prescribe the manner in which such acts, records, and proceedings shall be proved, and the effect thereof.

381. Before full faith and credit can be given to the public acts, records, and judicial proceedings of another state, it must first be shown that they are authentic; in other words, it must be shown that they are in fact such public acts, records, and judicial proceedings. The judgment of a state court, for example, when duly authenticated, must have full faith and credit given to it in every other court within the United States; but there must first be the authentication, or such effect does not follow.

382. It is left to Congress to prescribe the manner in which such acts, records, and proceedings shall be proved, and the effect of such proof. Congress have accordingly provided that the acts of the legislatures

of the several states shall be authenticated by having the seal of their respective states affixed thereto; and the records and judicial proceedings of their courts shall be proved or admitted in any other court within the United States by the attestation of the clerk and the seal of the court annexed, if there be a seal, together with a certificate of the judge, chief justice, or presiding magistrate, as the case may be, that the attestation is in due form.

383. Records and judicial proceedings, when thus authenticated, are to have such faith and credit given to them in every court within the United States as they have by law or usage in the courts of the state from whence they are taken.

384. Hence the judgment of a state court has the same credit, validity, and effect in every other court within the United States which it had in the state where it was rendered. The merits of the judgment cannot be re-examined. It may be shown, however, that it was obtained by fraud, or that the court rendering it had no jurisdiction, in which cases it is entitled to no faith or credit. Nor would it be entitled to any faith or credit out of the state in which it was rendered, if recovered against a non-resident party without notice to him.

Privileges of Citizens.

385. The citizens of each state are entitled to all privileges and immunities of citizens in the several states.

386. The privileges and immunities which are here secured to the citizens of each state in all the other states may be summed up as follows:—The right of a citizen of one state to pass through, or to reside in any other state, for purposes of trade, agriculture, professional pursuits, or otherwise; to claim the benefit of the writ of *habeas corpus;* to institute and maintain actions of any kind in the courts of the state; to take, hold, and dispose of property of every kind; to be exempted from higher taxes or impositions than are paid by the other citizens of the state; and to exercise the elective franchise as regulated and established by the laws or constitution of the state. In a word, the citizens of one state going into another are entitled to protection by the government of such state; to the enjoyment of life and liberty, and the pursuit of happiness, subject, however, to such restraints as the laws and Constitution may have prescribed for the general good of the whole.

386½. But a citizen of one state cannot claim any rights which under the laws of another state belong only to residents of the state. To enjoy such rights he must become domiciled there. He is, however, entitled to protection against any discriminating legislation which would place him in a worse situation than belongs to the proper citizen of the particular state. Hence a state license tax, which discriminates against commodities of other states is void, as abridging the privileges and immunities of the citizens of such other states. We may add, that the privileges and immunities referred to in the foregoing clause are those which belong to the citizens of the states as such, and are left to the state governments for security and protection, and are beyond the scope of the legislative and constitutional power of the government of the United States. We may add further, that the right to admittance to practice law in the courts of a state is not one of the privileges and immunities which a state is forbidden to abridge.

Fugitives from Justice.

387. A person charged in any state with treason, felony, or other crime, who shall flee from justice, and be found in another state, shall, on demand of the executive authority of the state from which he fled, be delivered up to be removed to the state having jurisdiction of the crime.

388. It is a question upon which jurists differ,

whether it is the duty of a nation, in the absence of a positive engagement, to surrender fugitives from justice who have sought shelter within its limits. It might, perhaps, be clearly implied that, in such a union of states as ours, every state is bound to deny an asylum to the criminals of the other states. But the Constitution has not left so important a question to inference or implication; it has enjoined it as a mutual obligation upon the states to deliver up, on demand, fugitives from justice. And Congress by law have prescribed the mode of proceeding when a fugitive from justice is demanded.

388½. The words "treason, felony, or other crime" include every offence forbidden and made punishable by the laws of the state where the offence is committed. And it must appear from the papers that the alleged fugitive committed the crime with which he is charged in the state from which the requisition proceeds. The obligation to surrender fugitives from justice rests upon the mutual good will and good faith of the states; and, hence, if the governor of a state should refuse on proper demand to deliver up such fugitive, the Federal courts have no power to compel him to perform the duty.

Fugitives from Labor.

389. No person held to service or labor in one state, under the laws thereof, escaping into another,

shall, in consequence of any law or regulation therein, be discharged from such service or labor, but shall be delivered up on claim of the party to whom such service or labor may be due.

390. Before the adoption of the Constitution, a slave escaping from one state into another could only be recovered as a matter of comity and favor, not as a matter of right. Because, by the law of nations, no independent state is bound to recognise the state of slavery as to foreign slaves found within its territory, when such recognition is in opposition to its own policy and institutions.

391. Hence the constitutional provision which makes that a matter of legal right which before could be claimed only as a matter of favor. Under the Constitution, therefore, a fugitive from service or labor cannot, in consequence of any law or regulation of the state into which he may have fled, be discharged from such service or labor, but must be delivered up on claim of the party entitled to his service or labor.

392. There must, however, be an *escape*. The Constitution does not extend to the case of a slave voluntarily carried by his master into a state in which slavery is not tolerated, or who goes there with his master's permission, and then escapes or refuses to return. Whether such a person shall be

delivered up, or be deemed free, depends wholly upon the local law and regulations, and not at all upon the Constitution or laws of the United States. Happily all questions growing out of the state of slavery are now at an end by its entire abolition.

NEW STATES AND TERRITORIES.

Admission of New States into the Union.

393. New states may be admitted by Congress into the Union; but no new state can be formed or erected within the jurisdiction of any other state; nor any state be formed by the junction of two or more states or parts of states, without the consent of the legislatures of the states concerned, as well as of the Congress.

394. At the time of the adoption of the Constitution, the United States possessed a vast extent of vacant territory which had been acquired, along with our independence, from England. We have since obtained immense acquisitions of territory from France, Spain, Mexico, and Russia; from France — the territory known as Louisiana; from Spain — Florida; and from Mexico — California, New Mexico, Utah, and extensive districts of country lying along the southern boundary of the United States; and from Russia — Alaska.

395. Out of these various acquisitions twenty-three

new states have already been admitted into the Union, originally composed of thirteen states; and territory yet remains sufficient when peopled to form perhaps fifteen or twenty more.

396. The usual mode of proceeding in the creation and admission of new states is as follows: When a territory has acquired such a population as fits it to become a state, the territorial legislature, with the permission of Congress, pass a law authorizing a convention to be chosen for the purpose of forming a constitution and state government. The constitution when formed is submitted to Congress by the convention, with the request that the territory may be admitted into the Union as a state. If the constitution is found to be republican, and is approved, Congress admit it on an equal footing with the original states.

397. To prevent Congress from arbitrarily creating new states by the division of the larger states, or the junction of the smaller ones, or of parts of states, it is provided that such division or junction shall not take place without the consent of the legislatures of the states concerned.

Territories.

398. Congress have power to dispose of and make all needful rules and regulations respecting the terri-

tory or other property belonging to the United States; and nothing in the Constitution shall be so construed as to prejudice any claims of the United States, or of any particular state.

399. The term "territory," as here used, is merely descriptive of one kind of property, and is equivalent to the word lands. The power of Congress to "dispose of" the public lands is not limited to making sales: they may be leased. But no property belonging to the United States can be disposed of, except by the authority of Congress.

400. It is observable that the right to acquire territory is nowhere expressly granted in the Constitution: but the power to make war and treaties is granted, and from this results the power to acquire territory in either of those modes, that is, by war or treaty. And the right to govern would seem to be the inevitable consequence of the right to acquire territory.

401. Until the territories of the United States have such a population as fits them to become states; that is, according to the usual rule, until they have such a population as would entitle them to a Representative in Congress by the existing ratio of representation, Congress may govern them in such mode, within the scope of its constitutional powers, as it thinks proper, either directly, by its own legislation,

or by means of territorial governments—the latter being the usual mode. And all measures commenced and prosecuted with a design to subvert the territorial government, and to establish and put in force in its place a new government, without the consent of Congress, are unlawful.

402. But the people of any territory may peaceably meet together in primary assemblies, or in conventions chosen by such assemblies, for the purpose of petitioning Congress to abrogate the territorial government, and to admit them into the Union as an independent state, and if they accompany their petition with a constitution, framed and agreed to by their primary assemblies, or by a convention of delegates duly authorized, there is no objection to their power to do so, nor to any measures which may be taken to collect the sense of the people in respect to it: provided such measures be prosecuted in a peaceable manner, in subordination to the existing government, and in subserviency to the power of Congress to adopt, reject, or disregard them, at their pleasure.

GUARANTY OF REPUBLICAN GOVERNMENT.

Injunction respecting.

403. The United States shall guarantee to every state in the Union a republican form of government, and shall protect each of them against invasion, and on application of the legislature, or of the executive (when the legislature cannot be convened), against domestic violence.

404. A confederacy of states, founded on dissimilar principles, some of the states having a republican form of government, some an aristocratic form, and others a monarchical form, would be very apt, from opposing views and policy, to be discordant, and fall into distraction. To avoid such a condition of affairs, the Constitution has provided that in all the states of the Union a republican form of government must be maintained.

405. It has been justly remarked that the only restriction imposed on the states by this clause of the Constitution is, that they shall not exchange republican for anti-republican institutions. They may alter or amend their respective constitutions as they please, only they must take care and preserve

the republican form. If they should adopt aristocratic or monarchical systems, or such systems should be imposed on them by the violence of parties or factions, the government of the United States would be bound to interpose and restore the republican form.

405½. And the standard by which the question must be determined whether the actual government is republican in form or not, is, does it correspond with the governments in existence when the Constitution was adopted? When a state is admitted into the Union, Congress determines, by the fact of admission, that the government of such state is republican in form. If changes are afterwards made which do not essentially alter the character of such government, as it stood when the state was admitted into the Union, Congress cannot interpose, however distasteful such changes may be. But, it seems, by recent decisions of the Supreme Court of the United States, that if Congress should unjustly, erroneously, and arbitrarily determine and declare that a particular state government was not republican in form, and refuse thereupon to recognize it, the citizens of such state are without redress. The judicial tribunals, in political questions, accept and follow the conclusions of the political department.

406. The United States are also bound to protect each state from invasion; and also against domestic

violence, such as insurrection or rebellion, on application of the legislature, or of the executive when the legislature cannot be convened.

AMENDMENTS.

Mode of.

407. Congress, whenever two-thirds of both Houses deem it necessary, must propose amendments to the Constitution, or, on the application of the legislatures of two-thirds of the several states, must call a convention for proposing amendments, which, in either case, are valid to all intents and purposes, as part of the constitution, when ratified by the legislatures of three-fourths of the several states, or by conventions in three-fourths thereof, as the one or the other mode of ratification may be proposed by Congress; provided, that no amendment, which may be made prior to the year one thousand eight hundred and eight, shall, in any manner, affect the first and fourth clauses in the ninth section of the first Article; and that no state, without its consent, shall be deprived of its equal suffrage in the Senate.

408. As useful alterations in the Constitution might be suggested by experience, a mode is provided for making them. This mode combines two great advantages; that is, changes can be made, but without too much facility on the one hand, or too

much difficulty on the other. If changes are too easily made, there will be instability in the government; if with too great difficulty, the community may be deprived of the benefit of salutary reforms, or seek a remedy in revolution or civil dissension.

409. No amendments, it will be observed, can be made to the Constitution unless two-thirds of Congress propose them, or they are proposed by a convention called by Congress, on the application of two-thirds of the legislatures of the several states; and also, unless three-fourths of the states, either by their legislatures or by conventions called for that purpose, ratify them.

410. No amendment, made prior to the year 1808, could affect, in any manner, those clauses which relate to the migration or importation of such persons as the states might think proper to admit, and to the manner in which direct taxes should be laid: in other words, no changes could be made in those clauses which relate to the importation of slaves, or the apportionment of taxes, until after the year 1808. A permanent limitation upon the power of amendment is, that no state, without its consent, shall be deprived of its equal suffrage in the Senate. It should be observed that a proposed amendment to the Constitution need not be presented to the President for his approval.

PUBLIC DEBT, SUPREMACY OF THE CONSTITUTION, &c.

Public Debt.

411. All debts contracted and engagements entered into before the adoption of the Constitution, are as valid against the United States, under the Constitution, as under the Confederation.

412. When a nation changes one form of government for another, the government under the new form becomes liable for all the obligations of the preceding government. Hence the government of the United States under the Constitution necessarily became liable for the debts and engagements entered into by the government of the United States under the Confederation. The object of expressly asserting this principle of the law of nations in the Constitution itself was, doubtless, to allay any apprehensions that the public creditors might be supposed to feel.

Supremacy of the Constitution.

413. The Constitution and the laws of the United States made in pursuance of it, and all treaties made, or which shall be made, under the authority of the

United States, are the supreme law of the land; and the judges in every state are bound thereby, anything in the constitution or laws of any state to the contrary notwithstanding.

414. The propriety and the necessity of making the Constitution, and the laws passed in pursuance of it, the supreme law of the land, are very obvious. The very existence of the federal government depends upon it. If the powers conferred on that government could be overridden by contradictory powers in the several state governments, they might as well not have been conferred at all. Necessarily, therefore, powers conferred for national purposes must be supreme over those conferred for state purposes. But those powers cannot be exceeded. If Congress pass laws not in pursuance of the Constitution, they are void, and it is the duty of the judiciary to declare them void. And it is equally their duty to declare void acts of the state legislatures which are repugnant to the Constitution of the United States.

415. A treaty ratified with proper formalities is, by the Constitution, the supreme law of the land, and the courts have no power to examine into the authority of the persons by whom it was entered into on behalf of the foreign nation. Whenever a right grows out of, or is protected by, a treaty, it is sanctioned against all the laws and judicial decisions of

the states; and whoever may have this right, it is to be protected.

Oath of Office.

416. The Senators and Representatives before mentioned, and the members of the several state legislatures, and all executive and judicial officers, both of the United States and of the several states, are bound by oath or affirmation to support the Constitution; but no religious test can ever be required as a qualification to any office or public trust under the United States.

417. The solemn sanction of an oath or affirmation is required of all officers, legislative, executive, and judicial, both of the state and United States governments, in order to secure their faithful support of the Constitution. Members and officers of the state governments are bound to take this oath, because they have an important agency in carrying the Constitution into effect; the state legislatures, for example, elect the Senate; and the state courts may be called on to decide cases in which are involved questions arising out of the Constitution, laws, and treaties of the United States.

No Religious Test.

418. Religious tests as a qualification to any office or public trust under the United States are prohibited,

because the Constitution contemplates entire freedom of religious belief and worship. It, therefore, forbids any test or oath by which adherence to any particular sect or form of belief shall be made a qualification for office.

Ratification of the Constitution.

419. The last article of the Constitution is as follows:—The ratification of the conventions of nine states shall be sufficient for the establishment of this Constitution between the states so ratifying the same.

420. The ratification of all the states as a condition to the establishment of the Constitution, would have put it in the power of any one state to have defeated the wishes of all the others. If a simple majority of states had been sufficient, it might happen that seven of the smaller states would ratify it, while the six larger would reject it—the consequence being the dissolution of the original union and probable dissension between the unequal parts. The Convention, therefore, avoided the danger of requiring a unanimous ratification on the one hand, and a mere majority ratification on the other. As we have already seen, only eleven of the states ratified it in the first instance; Rhode Island and North Carolina not ratifying until the government had gone into operation.

AMENDMENTS TO THE CONSTITUTION.

History of.

421. The conventions of a number of the states having, at the time of adopting the Constitution, expressed a desire, in order to prevent misconstruction or abuse of its powers, that further declaratory and restrictive clauses should be added, something, in fact, in the nature of a bill of rights, Congress, at their first session in 1789, proposed ten articles as additional to and amendatory of the Constitution. These articles, having been ratified by the requisite number of states, that is, by three-fourths, became a part of the Constitution.

422. In 1794 another amendment (the eleventh) was proposed by Congress, and, in 1803, the twelfth. Both of these proposed amendments were ratified by the constitutional number of states, and, equally with the first ten articles, became a part of the Constitution. Subsequently, to wit, in 1865, the thirteenth amendment was adopted; in 1866 the fourteenth; and in 1869 the fifteenth.

Character of the Amendments.

423. It is well settled that the first twelve amendments to the Constitution have no application to the legislation of the states. They are exclusively limitations of the power of the general government, and were intended to prevent interference with the rights of the states and of their citizens.

Freedom of Religion, &c.

424. Article first of the amendments declares that Congress shall make no law respecting an establishment of religion, or prohibiting the free exercise thereof; or abridging the freedom of speech or of the press; or the right of the people peaceably to assemble and to petition the government for a redress of grievances.

425. The subject of religion is left exclusively to the state governments. Congress is prohibited to create a religious establishment, or to intermeddle with the free exercise of religion; nor can a religious test ever be required as a qualification for any office or public trust under the United States. The persecutions, intolerance, and jealousy which had ever marked the establishment of a state religion or a national church were, doubtless, among the efficient

reasons why the Constitution thus forbids any union of civil and ecclesiastical authority, or any alliance between church and state. It regards with equal eye all religious sects; and prohibits Congress from interfering with the freedom of public worship. The religious liberties of the people are left to the respective state constitutions and laws. Congress have nothing to do with the subject.

Freedom of Speech and of the Press.

426. When it is said that Congress shall make no law abridging the freedom of speech, or of the press, it is not meant that every man may, with impunity, speak or print whatever he pleases, no matter how false, immoral, and malicious such speech or writing may be; but only that no previous restraints shall be laid on speech or publication.

427. While, therefore, every citizen may, with entire freedom, speak, write, and publish his sentiments on all subjects, and while no law can rightfully be passed by Congress to restrain or abridge this freedom, he is, nevertheless, responsible for every abuse of it. If he speaks or publishes what injures any other person in his rights, person, property, or reputation, or disturbs the public peace, or corrupts the public morals, he is answerable in damages for the injury to the individual, and is punishable, criminally, for the injury to society.

Right of Petition.

428. The right of a people peaceably to assemble for the purpose of petitioning the government for a redress of grievances, would seem to be inherent. A denial of that right would be totally inconsistent with the spirit and genius of free institutions. The Constitution, however, with that caution which is equally observable in other provisions, expressly recognises the right, and prohibits any abridgment of it.

Right of the People to keep and bear Arms.

429. The second amendment is as follows: — A well regulated militia being necessary to the security of a free state, the right of the people to keep and bear arms shall not be infringed.

430. With arms in their hands, the people will not be likely to permit the overthrow of their institutions by the unscrupulous ambition of a civil magistrate or military chieftain. The very fact of their being armed will serve as a check to any arbitrary or forcible invasion of their constitutional rights. Besides, a well regulated militia prevents the necessity of keeping on foot a large standing army, which, in addition to the expense it entails, has ever been deemed dangerous to the liberties of a people.

Quartering Soldiers on Citizens.

431. The third amendment is, that no soldier shall, in time of peace, be quartered in any house, without the consent of the owner; nor in time of war, but in a manner to be prescribed by law.

432. This is to prevent the practice which has often prevailed in arbitrary governments, and particularly in times of violence, of billeting soldiers upon private citizens without regard to their consent or wishes. This is manifestly a great grievance, and, in time of peace, is prohibited. But in time of war it may be necessary; but the manner of doing it must be prescribed by law.

Search Warrants.

433. The fourth amendment provides that the right of the people to be secure in their persons, houses, papers, and effects, against unreasonable searches and seizures, shall not be violated; and no warrants shall issue but upon probable cause, supported by oath or affirmation, and particularly describing the place to be searched, and the persons or things to be seized.

434. This refers only to warrants and process issued under the authority of the United States, and

was doubtless intended to guard against the practice which formerly prevailed in England, in one class of cases, of issuing warrants in a general form, which authorized the officer to search houses and arrest persons, without naming any persons or places in particular. This was a sort of roving commission to the officer to search any place and arrest any person whom he might suspect of being the accused party. The King's Bench, in the time of Chief Justice Pratt, pronounced general warrants to be totally illegal, and Parliament subsequently passed resolutions against them; resolutions by which the personal liberty of the subject was confirmed, and the lawful secrets of business and friendship were rendered inviolable.

435. Under the Constitution of the United States a warrant cannot issue but upon probable cause, supported by oath or affirmation, and particularly describing the place to be searched, and the person or things to be seized. The warrant, and the complaint under oath upon which it is founded, must not only state the name of the party, but also the time, and place, and nature of the offence, with reasonable certainty.

Reserved Rights.

436. The fifth, sixth, seventh, and eighth amendments have already been considered, and it is unnecessary to recur to them again: (See sec. 351, 361,

365, 368.) The ninth Article declares that the enumeration in the Constitution of certain rights shall not be construed to deny or disparage others retained by the people.

437. It is often said that the expression of one thing is the exclusion of another; and Bacon remarks that enumeration weakens the force of a law in cases not enumerated. It was to prevent the application of maxims like these, that the Constitution expressly declares that the enumeration of certain rights shall not be construed to deny or disparage others retained by the people.

Powers not delegated reserved.

438. The tenth Article is as follows:—The powers not granted to the United States by the Constitution, nor prohibited by it to the states, are reserved to the states respectively, or to the people.

439. The government of the United States being a government of limited and enumerated powers, it would seem naturally to follow, that powers not conferred were withheld, and belonged to the states or to the people of the states. But to quiet the fears of those who thought differently, this amendment was proposed and adopted, by which it is in effect declared that the government of the United States

shall assume no powers beyond those which are granted.

440. The eleventh and twelfth amendments, which relate to the jurisdiction of the judiciary and the mode of electing the President and Vice-President, have been already considered under those heads. (See sec. 255 *et seq.*)

440¼. The thirteenth amendment declares that "neither slavery nor involuntary servitude, except as a punishment for crime, whereof the party shall have been duly convicted, shall exist within the United States, or any place subject to their jurisdiction." And the second clause of this amendment provides that "Congress shall have power to enforce this article by appropriate legislation."

Appropriate legislation, under the latter clause, would seem to be limited, strictly, to such legislation as is essential to accomplish the purpose of the first clause, to wit, the prevention of slavery or involuntary servitude in the United States. It cannot legitimately, under pretence of that purpose, authorize Congress to pass laws, for example, which perhaps might add to the privileges or enjoyments of the state of freedom, but which, according to the import and genius of our constitutional system, are the proper subject of local and state legislation.

440½. The first paragraph of the fourteenth amendment provides as follows: "All persons born or naturalized in the United States, and subject to the jurisdiction thereof, are citizens of the United States, and of the state wherein they reside. No state shall make or enforce any law which shall abridge the privileges or immunities of citizens of the United States; nor shall any state deprive any person of life, liberty or property, without due process of law, nor deny to any person within its jurisdiction the equal protection of the laws."

A person may be a citizen, that is, owe allegiance to the government and be entitled to protection from it, and yet not possess the qualifications required by law to do certain things that other citizens do. For example, the mere fact of citizenship does not entitle any person to exercise the right of suffrage. He must in addition to such fact possess the qualifications required by law as the condition of such exercise. Consequently when the first clause of the fourteenth amendment declares who shall be citizens of the United States and of the several states, it does not thereby confer on them the right to vote.

The privileges and immunities which the fourteenth article forbids the several states to abridge, are those belonging to citizens of the United States, and not to those of the several states. What these privileges and immunities are it would be difficult to determine in a general definition. Among them, however, may be included the right of the citizen to visit the seat of government, to assert any claim he may have upon the government, or to transact any business he may have with it, to seek its protection, to share its offices, to engage in administering its functions. He has the right of free access to its seaports, through which all operations of foreign commerce are conducted, to the sub-treasuries, land offices, and courts of justice in the several states. Another privilege of a citizen of the United States is to demand the protection of the Federal government over his life, liberty, and property when on the high seas, or within the jurisdiction of a foreign government. The right to peaceably assemble and petition for redress of grievances, the privilege of the writ of *habeas corpus*, are rights of the citizen guaranteed by the Federal Constitution. The right to use the navigable waters of the United States, however they may penetrate the territories of the several states, all rights secured to citizens by treaties with foreign nations, are dependent upon citizenship of the United States and not citizenship of a state. The clause we are considering does not, it seems, restrain a state from granting a monopoly for the carrying on of any lawful industrial business, (not injurious to the community, nor the proper subject of police regulation,) and prohibiting its exercise by others than the monopolists. Such a grant, it is held, does not abridge the privileges of citizens of the United States.*

* It is the right of the state courts to decide finally whether any such exclusive privileges are forbidden by the state Constitutions.

We do not deem it necessary to consider in detail the remaining paragraphs and clauses of the fourteenth amendment. They are explicit and speak for themselves. We need only add, that under the fifth paragraph, which gives Congress the power to enforce the provisions thereof by appropriate legislation, a very stringent act (approved April 20, 1871) has been passed, to which the reader is referred.

The fifteenth amendment is as follows: "The right of citizens of the United States to vote shall not be denied or abridged by the United States or by any state, on account of race, color, or previous condition of servitude. The Congress shall have power to enforce this article by appropriate legislation."

This amendment does not confer on Congress the power to regulate the suffrage laws of the several states. But whatever qualifications may be prescribed by those laws, or whatever inequalities may exist under them, or however the privilege of the ballot may be denied or abridged on other grounds, no qualification or inequality, or denial or abridgment of the elective franchise can be made on account of race, color, or previous condition of servitude.

Conclusion.

441. We have thus concluded our examination of the Constitution of the United States: Adopted at a time when public affairs were sinking into disorder and confusion, and when the firmest patriots had

begun to fear that the benefits of the revolutionary struggle were to be lost, it restored the public confidence, revived the public credit, and laid the foundations of order, stability, and unequalled prosperity. If we would preserve it, and transmit it as a rich heritage to posterity, an habitual reverence for it should be inculcated, and its principles be studied and maintained.

APPENDIX.

I.

THE DECLARATION OF INDEPENDENCE.

II.

THE ARTICLES OF CONFEDERATION.

III.

RESOLUTIONS AND LETTER TRANSMITTED TO CONGRESS BY THE FEDERAL CONVENTION.

IV.

WASHINGTON'S FAREWELL ADDRESS.

APPENDIX.

I.

A DECLARATION BY THE REPRESENTATIVES OF THE UNITED STATES OF AMERICA, IN CONGRESS ASSEMBLED.

When, in the course of human events, it becomes necessary for one people to dissolve the political bands which have connected them with another, and to assume, among the powers of the earth, the separate and equal station to which the laws of nature and of nature's God entitle them, a decent respect to the opinions of mankind requires that they should declare the causes which impel them to the separation.

We hold these truths to be self-evident, that all men are created equal; that they are endowed by their Creator with certain unalienable rights; that among these, are life, liberty, and the pursuit of happiness. That, to secure these rights, governments are instituted among men, deriving their just powers from the consent of the governed; that, whenever any form of government becomes destructive of these ends, it is the right of the people to alter or to abolish it, and to institute a new government, laying its foundation on such principles, and organizing its powers in such form, as to them shall seem most likely to effect their safety and happiness. Prudence, indeed, will dictate that governments long established, should not be changed for light and transient causes; and, accordingly, all experience hath shown, that mankind are more disposed to suffer, while evils are sufferable, than to right themselves by abolishing the forms to which they are accustomed. But, when a long train of abuses and usurpations, pursuing invariably the same object, evinces a design to reduce them under absolute despotism, it is their right, it is their duty, to throw off such government, and to provide new guards for their future security. Such has been the patient sufferance of these colonies, and such is now the necessity which constrains them to alter their former systems of government. The history of the present king of Great Britain is a history of repeated injuries and usurpations, all having, in direct object, the establishment of an absolute tyranny over these States. To prove this, let facts be submitted to a candid world:

He has refused his assent to laws the most wholesome and necessary for the public good.

He has forbidden his governors to pass laws of immediate and pressing importance, unless suspended in their operation till his assent should be obtained; and, when so suspended, he has utterly neglected to attend to them.

He has refused to pass other laws for the accommodation of large districts of people, unless those people would relinquish the right of representation in the legislature; a right inestimable to them, and formidable to tyrants only.

He has called together legislative bodies at places unusual, uncomfortable, and distant from the depository of their public records, for the sole purpose of fatiguing them into compliance with his measures.

He has dissolved representative houses repeatedly, for

opposing, with manly firmness, his invasions on the rights of the people.

He has refused, for a long time after such dissolutions, to cause others to be elected; whereby the legislative powers, incapable of annihilation, have returned to the people at large for their exercise; the State remaining, in the mean time, exposed to all the danger of invasion from without, and convulsions within.

He has endeavored to prevent the population of these States; for that purpose, obstructing the laws for naturalization of foreigners; refusing to pass others to encourage their migration hither, and raising the conditions of new appropriations of lands.

He has obstructed the administration of justice, by refusing his assent to laws for establishing judiciary powers.

He has made judges dependent on his will alone, for the tenure of their offices, and the amount and payment of their salaries.

He has erected a multitude of new offices, and sent hither swarms of officers to harass our people, and eat out their substance.

He has kept among us, in times of peace, standing armies, without the consent of our legislature.

He has affected to render the military independent of, and superior to, the civil power.

He has combined, with others, to subject us to a jurisdiction foreign to our constitution, and unacknowledged by our laws; giving his assent to their acts of pretended legislation:

For quartering large bodies of armed troops among us:

For protecting them, by a mock trial, from punishment, for any murders which they should commit on the inhabitants of these States:

For cutting off our trade with all parts of the world:

For imposing taxes on us without our consent:

For depriving us, in many cases, of the benefits of trial by jury:

For transporting us beyond seas to be tried for pretended offences:

For abolishing the free system of English laws in a neighboring province, establishing therein an arbitrary government, and enlarging its boundaries, so as to render it at once an example and fit instrument for introducing the same absolute rule into these colonies:

For taking away our charters, abolishing our most valuable laws, and altering, fundamentally, the powers of our governments:

For suspending our own legislatures, and declaring themselves invested with power to legislate for us in all cases whatsoever.

He has abdicated government here, by declaring us out of his protection, and waging war against us.

He has plundered our seas, ravaged our coasts, burnt our towns, and destroyed the lives of our people.

He is, at this time, transporting large armies of foreign mercenaries to complete the works of death, desolation, and tyranny, already begun, with circumstances of cruelty and perfidy scarcely paralleled in the most barbarous ages, and totally unworthy the head of a civilized nation.

He has constrained our fellow-citizens, taken captive on the high seas, to bear arms against their country, to become the executioners of their friends and brethren, or to fall themselves by their hands.

He has excited domestic insurrections amongst us, and has endeavored to bring on the inhabitants of our frontiers, the merciless Indian savages, whose known rule of warfare is an undistinguished destruction, of all ages, sexes, and conditions.

In every stage of these oppressions, we have petitioned for redress, in the most humble terms; our repeated petitions have been answered only by repeated injury. A prince, whose character is thus marked by every act which may define a tyrant, is unfit to be the ruler of a free people.

Nor have we been wanting in attention to our British brethren.

We have warned them, from time to time, of attempts made by their legislature to extend an unwarrantable jurisdiction over us. We have reminded them of the circumstances of our emigration and settlement here. We have appealed to their native justice and magnanimity, and we have conjured them, by the ties of our common kindred, to disavow these usurpations, which would inevitably interrupt our connections and correspondence. They, too, have been deaf to the voice of justice and consanguinity. We must, therefore, acquiesce in the necessity which denounces our separation, and hold them as we hold the rest of mankind, enemies in war, in peace, friends.

We, therefore, the representatives of the UNITED STATES OF AMERICA, in GENERAL CONGRESS assembled, appealing to the Supreme Judge of the world for the rectitude of our intentions, do, in the name, and by the authority of the good people of these colonies, solemnly publish and declare, That these United Colonies are, and of right ought to be, *free and independent States;* that they are absolved from all allegiance to the British crown, and that all political connection between them and the state of Great Britain, is, and ought to be, totally dissolved; and that, as FREE AND INDEPENDENT STATES, they have full power to levy war, conclude peace, contract alliances, establish commerce, and to do all other acts and things which INDEPENDENT STATES may of right do. And, for the support of this declaration,

22

with a firm reliance on the protection of DIVINE PROVIDENCE, we mutually pledge to each other, our lives, our fortunes, and our sacred honor.

JOHN HANCOCK.

New Hampshire.

Josiah Bartlett,
William Whipple,
Matthew Thornton.

Massachusetts Bay.

Samuel Adams,
John Adams,
Robert Treat Paine,
Elbridge Gerry.

Rhode Island.

Stephen Hopkins,
William Ellery.

Connecticut.

Roger Sherman,
Samuel Huntington,
William Williams,
Oliver Wolcott.

New York.

William Floyd,
Philip Livingston,
Francis Lewis,
Lewis Morris.

New Jersey.

Richard Stockton,
John Witherspoon,
Francis Hopkinson,
John Hart,
Abraham Clark.

Pennsylvania.

Robert Morris,
Benjamin Rush,
Benjamin Franklin,
John Morton,
George Clymer,
James Smith,
George Taylor,
James Wilson,
George Ross.

Delaware.

Cæsar Rodney,
George Read,
Thomas M'Kean.

Maryland.

Samuel Chase,
William Paca,
Thomas Stone,
Charles Carroll, of Carrollton.

Virginia.

George Wythe,
Richard Henry Lee,
Thomas Jefferson,
Benjamin Harrison,

THOMAS NELSON, JR.
FRANCIS LIGHTFOOT LEE,
CARTER BRAXTON.

North Carolina.

WILLIAM HOOPER,
JOSEPH HEWES,
JOHN PENN.

South Carolina.

EDWARD RUTLEDGE,
THOMAS HEYWARD, JR.,
THOMAS LYNCH, JR.,
ARTHUR MIDDLETON.

Georgia.

BUTTON GWINNETT,
LYMAN HALL,
GEO. WALTON.

II.

ARTICLES OF CONFEDERATION

And perpetual union between the states of New Hampshire, Massachusetts Bay, Rhode Island and Providence Plantations, Connecticut, New York, New Jersey, Pennsylvania, Delaware, Maryland, Virginia, North Carolina, South Carolina, and Georgia.

ARTICLE I. The style of this Confederacy shall be, "THE UNITED STATES OF AMERICA."

ARTICLE II. Each state retains its sovereignty, freedom, and independence, and every power, jurisdiction, and right, which is not by this Confederation expressly delegated to the United States in Congress assembled.

ARTICLE III. The said states hereby severally enter into a firm league of friendship with each other, for their common defence, the security of their liberties, and their mutual and general welfare; binding themselves to assist each other against all force offered to, or attacks made upon them, or any of them, on account of religion, sovereignty, trade, or any other pretence whatever.

Article IV. The better to secure and perpetuate mutual friendship and intercourse among the people of the different states in this Union, the free inhabitants of each of these states, paupers, vagabonds, and fugitives from justice excepted, shall be entitled to all privileges and immunities of free citizens in the several states; and the people of each state shall have free ingress and regress to and from any other state; and shall enjoy therein all the privileges of trade and commerce, subject to the same duties, impositions, and restrictions as the inhabitants thereof respectively; provided, that such restriction shall not extend so far as to prevent the removal of property imported into any state to any other state, of which the owner is an inhabitant; provided also, that no imposition, duties, or restriction shall be laid by any state on the property of the United States, or either of them.

If any person guilty of, or charged with treason, felony, or other high misdemeanor, in any state, shall flee from justice, and be found in any of the United States, he shall, upon demand of the governor or executive power of the state from which he fled, be delivered up and removed to the state having jurisdiction of his offence.

Full faith and credit shall be given in each of these states to the records, acts, and judicial proceedings of the courts and magistrates of every other state.

Article V. For the more convenient management of the general interests of the United States, delegates shall be annually appointed in such manner as the legislature of each state shall direct, to meet in Congress on the first Monday in November, in every year, with a power reserved to each state to recall its delegates, or any of them, at any time within the year, and send others in their stead for the remainder of the year.

No state shall be represented in Congress by less than two, nor by more than seven members; and no person shall be capable of being a delegate for more than three years in any term of six years; nor shall any person, being a delegate, be capable of holding any office under the United States, for which he, or another for his benefit, receives any salary, fees, or emolument of any kind.

Each state shall maintain its own delegates in a meeting of the states, and while they act as members of the committee of the states.

In determining questions in the United States in Congress assembled, each state shall have one vote.

Freedom of speech and debate in Congress shall not be impeached or questioned in any court or place out of Congress; and the members of Congress shall be protected in their persons from arrests and imprisonment during the time of their going to, and from, and attending on Congress, except for treason, felony, or breach of the peace.

Article VI. No state, without the consent of the United States in Congress assembled, shall send any embassy to, or receive any embassy from, or enter into any conference, agreement, alliance, or treaty with any king, prince, or state; nor shall any person, holding any office of profit or trust under the United States, or any of them, accept of any present, emolument, office, or title of any kind whatever from any king, prince, or foreign state; nor shall the United States in Congress assembled, or any of them, grant any title of nobility.

No two or more states shall enter into any treaty, confederation, or alliance whatever between them, without the consent of the United States in Congress assembled, specifying accurately the purposes for which the same is to be entered into, and how long it shall continue.

No state shall lay any imposts or duties, which may interfere with any stipulations in treaties entered into by the United States in Congress assembled with any king, prince, or state, in pursuance of any treaties already proposed by Congress to the Courts of France and Spain.

No vessels of war shall be kept up, in time of peace, by any state, except such number only as shall be deemed necessary, by the United States in Congress assembled, for the defence of such state or its trade; nor shall any body of forces be kept up by any state, in time of peace, except such number only as, in the judgment of the United States in Congress assembled, shall be deemed requisite to garrison the forts necessary for the defence of such state: but every state shall always keep up a well-regulated and disciplined militia, sufficiently armed and accoutred; and shall provide and constantly have ready for use, in public stores, a due number of field-pieces and tents, and a proper quantity of arms, ammunition, and camp equipage.

No state shall engage in any war, without the consent of the United States in Congress assembled, unless such state be actually invaded by enemies, or shall have received certain advice of a resolution being formed by some nation of Indians to invade such state, and the danger is so imminent as not to admit of a delay till the United States in Congress assembled can be consulted; nor shall any state grant commissions to any ship or vessels of war, nor letters of marque or reprisal, except it be after a declaration of war by the United States in Congress assembled; and then only against the kingdom or state, and the subjects thereof, against which war has been so declared, and under such regulations as shall be established by the United States in Congress assembled, unless such state be infested by pirates, in which case vessels of war may be fitted out for that occasion, and kept so long as the danger shall continue, or until the United States in Congress assembled shall determine otherwise.

Article VII. When land forces are raised by any state for the common defence, all officers of or under the rank of colonel shall be appointed by the legislature of each state respectively, by whom such forces shall be raised, or in such manner as such state shall direct; and all vacancies shall be filled up by the state which first made the appointment.

Article VIII. All charges of war, and all other expenses that shall be incurred for the common defence or general welfare, and allowed by the United States in Congress assembled, shall be defrayed out of a common treasury which shall be supplied by the several states in proportion to the value of all land within each state, granted to or surveyed for any person as such land and the buildings and improvements thereon shall be estimated, according to such mode as the United States in Congress assembled shall, from time to time, direct and appoint. The taxes for paying that proportion shall be laid and levied by the authority and direction of the legislatures of the several states, within the time agreed upon by the United States in Congress assembled.

Article IX. The United States, in Congress assembled, shall have the sole and exclusive right and power of determining on peace and war, except in the cases mentioned in the sixth Article: Of sending and receiving ambassadors: Entering into treaties and alliances, provided that no treaty of commerce shall be made whereby the legislative power of the respective states shall be restrained from imposing such imposts and duties on foreigners as their own people are subjected to, or from prohibiting the exportation or importation of any species of goods or commodities whatever: Of establishing rules for deciding, in all cases, what captures on land or water shall be legal; and in what manner prizes, taken by land or naval forces in the service of the United States, shall be divided or appropriated: Of granting letters of marque and reprisal in times of peace: Appointing courts for the trial of piracies and felonies committed on the high seas; and establishing courts for receiving and determining, finally, appeals in all cases of captures; provided that no member of Congress shall be appointed a judge of any of the said courts.

The United States, in Congress assembled, shall also be the last resort, on appeal, in all disputes and differences now subsisting, or that hereafter may arise between two or more states concerning boundary, jurisdiction, or any other cause whatever; which authority shall always be exercised in the manner following: Whenever the legislative or executive authority, or lawful agent of any state, in controversy with another, shall present a petition to Congress, stating the matter in question, and praying for a hearing, notice thereof shall be given, by order of Congress, to the legislative or executive authority of the other state in controversy; and a day assigned for the appearance of the parties by their lawful agents, who shall then be directed to appoint, by joint consent, commissioners or judges to constitute a court for hearing and determining the matter in question: but if they cannot agree, Congress shall name three persons out of each of the United States; and from the list of such persons each party shall alternately strike out one, the petitioners beginning, until the number shall be reduced to thirteen; and from that number not less than seven nor more than nine names, as Congress shall direct, shall, in the presence of Congress, be drawn out by lot; and the persons whose names shall be so drawn, or any five of them, shall be commissioners or judges to hear and finally determine the controversy, so always as a major part of the judges, who shall hear the cause, shall agree in the determination. And if either party shall neglect to attend at the day appointed, without showing reasons which Congress shall judge sufficient, or being present shall refuse to strike, the Congress shall proceed to nominate three persons out of each state, and the Secretary of Congress shall strike in behalf of such party absent or refusing; and the judgment and sentence of the court, to be appointed in the manner before prescribed, shall be final and conclusive. And if any of the parties shall refuse to submit to the authority of such court, or to appear, or defend their claim or cause, the court shall nevertheless proceed to pronounce sentence or judgment, which shall in like manner be final and decisive; the judgment or sentence and other proceedings being, in either case, transmitted to Congress and lodged among the Acts of Congress for the security of the parties concerned: Provided that every commissioner, before he sits in judgment, shall take an oath, to be administered by one of the judges of the supreme or superior court of the state where the cause shall be tried, "Well and truly to hear and determine the matter in question, according to the best of his judgment, without favor, affection, or hope of reward:" Provided also, that no state shall be deprived of territory for the benefit of the United States.

All controversies concerning the private right of soil claimed under different grants of two or more states, whose jurisdictions, as they may respect such lands and the states which passed such grants, are adjusted, the said grants, or either of them, being at the same time claimed to have originated antecedent to such settlement of jurisdiction, shall, on the petition of either party to the Congress of the United States, be finally determined, as near as may be, in the same manner as is before prescribed for deciding disputes respecting territorial jurisdiction between different states.

The United States, in Congress assembled, shall also have the sole and exclusive right and power of regulating the alloy and value of coin struck by their own authority, or by that of the respective states: Fixing the standard of weights and measures throughout the United States: Regulating the trade and managing all affairs with the Indians, not members of any of the states; provided that the legislative right of any state within its own limits be not infringed or violated: Establishing and regulating post-offices, from one state to another, throughout all the United States, and exacting such postage on the papers passing through the same as may be requisite to defray the expenses of the said office: Appointing all officers of the land forces in the service of the United States, excepting regimental officers: Appointing all the officers of the naval forces, and commissioning all officers whatever in the service of the United States: Making rules for the government and regulation of the land and naval forces, and directing their operations.

The United States, in Congress assembled, shall have authority to appoint a committee, to sit in the recess of Congress, to be denominated A COMMITTEE OF THE STATES, and to consist of one delegate from each state, and to appoint such other committees and civil officers as may be necessary for managing the general affairs of the United States under their direction: To appoint one of their number to preside; provided that no person be allowed to serve in the office of president more than one year in any term of three years: To ascertain the necessary sums of money to be raised for the service of the United States, and to appropriate and apply the same for defraying the public expenses: To borrow money or emit bills on the credit of the United States, transmitting every half year to the respective states an account of the sums of money so borrowed or emitted: To build and equip a navy: To agree upon the number of land forces, and to make requisitions from each state for its quota, in proportion to the number of white inhabitants in such state, which requisition shall be binding; and thereupon the legislature of each state shall appoint the regimental officers, raise the men, and clothe, arm, and equip them, in a soldierlike manner, at the expense of the United States; and the officers and men so clothed, armed, and equipped, shall march to the place appointed, and within the time agreed on by the United States in Congress assembled: but if the United States, in Congress assembled, shall, on consideration of circumstances, judge proper that any state should not raise men, or should raise a smaller number than its quota, and that any other state should raise a greater number of men than its quota thereof, such extra number shall be raised, officered, clothed, armed, and equipped in the same manner as the quota of such state; unless the legislature of such state shall judge that such extra number cannot be safely spared out of the same; in which case they shall raise, officer, clothe, arm, and equip as many of such extra number as they judge can be safely spared: and the officers and men so clothed, armed, and equipped, shall march to the place appointed, and within the time agreed on by the United States in Congress assembled.

The United States, in Congress assembled, shall never engage in a war; nor grant letters of marque and reprisal in time of peace; nor enter into any treaties or alliances; nor coin money; nor regulate the value thereof; nor ascertain the sums and expenses necessary for the defence and welfare of the United States, or any of them; nor emit bills; nor borrow money on the credit of the United States; nor appropriate money; nor agree upon the number of vessels of war to be built or purchased, or the number of land or sea forces to be raised; nor appoint a Commander-in-Chief of the army or navy; unless nine states assent to the same; nor shall a question on any other point, except for adjourning from day to day, be determined, unless by the votes of a majority of the United States in Congress assembled.

The Congress of the United States shall have power to adjourn to any time within the year, and to any place within the United States, so that no period of adjournment be for a longer duration than the space of six months; and shall publish the Journal of their proceedings monthly, except such parts thereof relating to treaties, alliances, or military operations, as in their judgment require secrecy; and the yeas and nays of the delegates of each state on any question shall be entered on the Journal, when it is desired by any delegate; and the delegates of a state, or any of them, at his or their request shall be furnished with a transcript of the said Journal, except such parts as are above excepted, to lay before the legislatures of the several states.

Article X. The committee of the states, or any nine of them, shall be authorized to execute, in the recess of Congress, such of the powers of Congress as the United States in Congress assembled, by the consent of nine states, shall from time to time think expedient to vest them with; provided that no power be delegated to the said committee, for the exercise of which, by the Articles of Confederation, the voice of nine states in the Congress of the United States assembled is requisite.

Article XI. Canada, acceding to this Confederation, and joining in the measures of the United States, shall be admitted into, and entitled to all the advantages of this Union; but no other colony shall be admitted into the same, unless such admission be agreed to by nine states.

Article XII. All bills of credit emitted, moneys borrowed, and debts contracted by, or under the authority of Congress, before the assembling of the United States, in pursuance of the present Confederation, shall be deemed and considered as a charge against the United States, for payment and satisfaction whereof the said United States, and the public faith, are hereby solemnly pledged.

ARTICLE XIII. Every state shall abide by the determinations of the United States in Congress assembled, on all questions which by this Confederation are submitted to them. And the Articles of this Confederation shall be inviolably observed by every state; and the Union shall be perpetual. Nor shall any alteration at any time hereafter be made in any of them, unless such alteration be agreed to in a Congress of the United States, and be afterwards confirmed by the legislatures of every state.

And whereas, it hath pleased the Great Governor of the world to incline the hearts of the legislatures we respectively represent in Congress, to approve of, and to authorize us to ratify the said Articles of Confederation and perpetual Union: Know ye that we the undersigned delegates, by virtue of the power and authority to us given for that purpose, do by these presents, in the name and in behalf of our respective constituents, fully and entirely ratify and confirm each and every of the said Articles of Confederation and perpetual Union, and all and singular the matters and things therein contained. And we do further solemnly plight and engage the faith of our respective constituents, that they shall abide by the determinations of the United States in Congress assembled, on all questions, which by the said Confederation are submitted to them; and that the articles thereof shall be inviolably observed by the states we respectively represent; and that the Union shall be perpetual. In witness whereof we have hereunto set our hands in Congress. Done at Philadelphia, in the state of

Pennsylvania, the 9th day of July, in the year of our Lord 1778, and in the 3d year of the Independence of America.

III.

IN CONVENTION, MONDAY, SEPTEMBER 17, 1787.

Present: The States of New Hampshire, Massachusetts, Connecticut, Mr. Hamilton from New York, New Jersey, Pennsylvania, Delaware, Maryland, Virginia, North Carolina, South Carolina, and Georgia.

Resolved, That the preceding Constitution be laid before the United States in Congress assembled, and that it is the opinion of this convention that it should afterwards be submitted to a Convention of delegates, chosen in each state by the people thereof, under the recommendation of its legislature, for their assent and ratification; and that each convention, assenting to and ratifying the same, should give notice thereof, to the United States in Congress assembled.

Resolved, That it is the opinion of this Convention, that as soon as the conventions of nine states shall have ratified this Constitution, the United States in Congress assembled should fix a day on which electors should be appointed by the states which shall have ratified the same, and a day on which the electors should assemble to vote for the President, and the time and place for commencing proceedings under this Constitution. That after such publication the electors should be appointed, and the Senators and Representatives elected; that the electors should meet on the day fixed for the election of the President, and should transmit their votes certified, signed, sealed, and directed as the Constitution requires, to the Secretary of the United States in Congress assembled; that the Senators and Representatives should convene at the time and place assigned; that the Senators should appoint a president of the Senate, for the sole purpose of receiving, opening, and counting the votes for President; and that, after he shall be chosen, the Congress, together with the President, should, without delay, proceed to execute this Constitution.

By the unanimous order of the Convention.

GEORGE WASHINGTON, *President.*

WILLIAM JACKSON, *Secretary.*

IN CONVENTION, SEPTEMBER 17, 1787.

SIR: We have now the honor to submit to the consideration of the United States in Congress assembled, that Constitution which has appeared to us the most advisable.

The friends of our country have long seen and desired that the power of making war, peace, and treaties, that of levying money and regulating commerce, and the correspondent executive and judicial authorities, should be fully and effectually vested in the General Government of the Union; but the impropriety of delegating such extensive trust to one body of men is evident: hence results the necessity of a different organization.

It is obviously impracticable, in the Federal Government of these States, to secure all rights of independent sovereignty to each, and yet provide for the interest and safety of all. Individuals entering into society must give up a share of liberty to preserve the rest. The magnitude of the sacrifice must depend as well on situation and circumstance as on the object to be obtained. It is at all times difficult to draw with precision the line between those rights which must be surrendered and those which may be reserved; and on the present occasion this difficulty was increased by a difference among the several states as to their situation, extent, habits, and particular interests.

In all our deliberations on this subject, we kept steadily in our view that which appears to us the greatest interest of every true American—the consolidation of our Union—in which is involved our prosperity, felicity, safety, perhaps our national existonce. This important consideration, seriously and deeply impressed on our minds, led each state in the Convention to be less rigid on points of inferior magnitude than might have been otherwise expected; and thus the Constitution which we now present is the result of a spirit of amity, and of that mutual deference and concession which the peculiarity of our political situation rendered indispensable.

That it will meet the full and entire approbation of every state, is not, perhaps, to be expected; but each will doubtless consider that, had her interest been alone consulted, the consequences might have been particularly disagreeable or injurious to others; that it is liable to as few exceptions as could reasonably have been expected, we hope and believe; that it may promote the lasting welfare of that country so dear to us all, and secure her freedom and happiness, is our most ardent wish.

With great respect, we have the honor to be, sir, your excellency's most obedient, humble servants.

By unanimous order of the Convention.

GEORGE WASHINGTON, *President.*

His Excellency the PRESIDENT OF CONGRESS.

IV.

WASHINGTON'S FAREWELL ADDRESS TO THE PEOPLE OF THE UNITED STATES, SEPTEMBER 17, 1796.

Friends and Fellow-citizens:—

The period for a new election of a citizen to administer the Executive Government of the United States being not far distant, and the time actually arrived, when your thoughts must be employed in designating the person who is to be clothed with that important trust, it appears to me proper, especially as it may conduce to a more distinct expression of the public voice, that I should now apprise you of the resolution I have formed, to decline being considered among the number of those out of whom a choice is to be made.

I beg you, at the same time, to do me the justice to be assured, that this resolution has not been taken, without a strict regard to all the considerations appertaining to the relation which binds a dutiful citizen to his country; and that, in withdrawing the tender of service, which silence, in my situation, might imply, I am influenced by no diminution of zeal for your future interest; no deficiency of grateful respect for your past kindness; but am supported by a full conviction that the step is compatible with both.

The acceptance of, and continuance hitherto in, the office to which your suffrages have twice called me, have been a uniform sacrifice of inclination to the opinion of duty, and to a deference for what appeared to be your desire. I constantly hoped that it would have been much earlier in my power, consistently with motives which I was not at liberty to disregard, to return to that retirement from which I had been reluctantly drawn. The strength of my inclination to do this, previous to the last election, had even led to the preparation of an address, to declare it to you; but mature reflection on the then perplexed and critical posture of our affairs with foreign nations, and the unanimous advice of persons entitled to my confidence, impelled me to abandon the idea.

I rejoice that the state of your concerns, external as well as internal, no longer renders the pursuit of inclination incompatible with the sentiment of duty or propriety; and am persuaded, whatever partiality may be retained for my services, that, in the present circumstances of our country, you will not disapprove my determination to retire.

The impressions, with which I first undertook the arduous trust, were explained on the proper occasion. In the discharge of this trust, I will only say, that I have, with good intentions, contributed towards the organization and administration of the Government, the best exertions of which a very fallible judgment was capable. Not unconscious, in the outset, of the inferiority of my qualifications, experience in my own eyes, perhaps still more in the eyes of others, has strengthened the motives to diffidence of myself; and, every day, the increasing weight of years admonishes me, more and more, that the shade of retirement is as necessary to me as it will be welcome. Satisfied that, if any circumstances have given peculiar value to my services, they were temporary, I have the consolation to believe, that, while choice and prudence invite me to quit the political scene, patriotism does not forbid it.

In looking forward to the moment which is intended to terminate the career of my public life, my feelings do not permit me to suspend the deep acknowledgment of that debt of gratitude which I owe to my beloved country, for the many honors it has conferred upon me; still more for the steadfast confidence with which it has supported me; and for the opportunities I have thence enjoyed, of manifesting my inviolable attachment, by services faithful and persevering, though in usefulness unequal to my zeal. If benefits have resulted to our country from these services, let it always be remembered to your praise, and as an instructive example in our annals, that, under circumstances in which the passions, agitated in every direction, were liable to mislead, amidst appearances sometimes dubious, vicissitudes of fortune often discouraging, in situations in which, not unfrequently, want of success has countenanced the spirit of criticism, the constancy of your support was the essential prop of the efforts, and a guarantee of the plans, by which they were effected. Profoundly penetrated with this idea, I shall carry it with me to my grave, as a strong incitement to unceasing vows, that Heaven may continue to you the choicest tokens of its beneficence; that your union and brotherly affection may be perpetual; that the free Constitution, which is the work of your hands, may be sacredly maintained; that its administration, in every department, may be stamped with wisdom and virtue; that, in fine, the happiness of the people of these states, under the auspices of liberty, may be made complete by so careful a preservation, and so prudent a use of this blessing, as will acquire to them the glory of recommending it to the applause, the affection, and adoption, of every nation which is yet a stranger to it.

Here, perhaps, I ought to stop; but a solicitude for your welfare, which cannot end but with my life, and the apprehension of danger, natural to that solicitude, urge me, on an occasion like the present, to offer to your solemn contemplation, and to recommend to your frequent review, some sentiments which are the result of much reflection; of no inconsiderable observation; and which appear to me all important to the permanency of your felicity as a people. These will be offered to you with the more freedom, as you can only see in them the disinterested warnings of a parting friend, who can possibly have no personal motive to bias his counsel; nor can I forget, as an encouragement to it, your indulgent reception of my sentiments on a former, and not dissimilar, occasion.

Interwoven as is the love of liberty with every ligament of your hearts, no recommendation of mine is necessary to fortify, or confirm, the attachment.

The unity of government, which constitutes you one people, is also now dear to you. It is justly so; for it is a main pillar in the edifice of your real independence; the support of your tranquillity at home, your peace abroad; of your safety; of your prosperity; of that very liberty which you so highly prize. But, as it is easy to foresee, that, from different causes, and from different quarters, much pains will be taken, many artifices employed, to weaken, in your minds, the conviction of this truth; as this is the point in your political fortress, against which the batteries of internal and external enemies will be most constantly and actively (though often covertly and insidiously) directed, it is of infinite moment that you should properly estimate the immense value of your National Union, to your collective and individual happiness; that you should cherish a cordial, habitual, and immovable attachment to it; accustoming yourselves to think and speak of it as of the palladium of your political safety and prosperity; watching for its preservation with jealous anxiety; discountenancing whatever may suggest even a suspicion that it can, in any event, be abandoned; and indignantly frowning upon the first dawning of every attempt to alienate any portion of our country from the rest, or to enfeeble the sacred ties which now link together the various parts.

For this you have every inducement of sympathy and interest. Citizens, by birth or choice, of a common country, that country has a right to concentrate your affections. The name of AMERICAN, which belongs to you in your national capacity, must always exalt the just pride of patriotism, more than any appellation derived from local discriminations. With slight shades of difference, you have the same religion, manners, habits, and political principles. You have, in a common cause, fought and triumphed together: the independence and liberty you possess are the work of joint councils and joint efforts, of common dangers, sufferings, and successes.

But these considerations, however powerfully they address themselves to your sensibility, are greatly outweighed by those which apply more immediately to your interest. Here every portion of our country finds the most commanding motives for carefully guarding and preserving the union of the whole.

The North, in an unrestrained intercourse with the South, protected by the equal laws of a common Government, finds, in the productions of the latter, great additional resources of maritime and commercial enterprise, and precious materials of manufacturing industry. The South, in the same intercourse, benefiting by the agency of the North, sees its agriculture grow, and its commerce expand. Turning partly into its own channels the seamen of the North, it finds its particular navigation invigorated: and, while it contributes, in different ways, to nourish and increase the general mass of the national navigation, it looks forward to the protection of a maritime strength, to which itself is unequally adapted. The East, in like intercourse with the West, already finds, and in the progressive improvement of interior communications, by land and water, will more and more find, a valuable vent for the commodities which it brings from abroad, or manufactures at home. The West derives from the East supplies requisite to its growth and comfort; and, what is, perhaps, of still greater consequence, it must, of necessity, owe the secure enjoyment of indispensable *outlets* for its own productions, to the weight, influence, and the future maritime strength of the Atlantic side of the Union, directed by an indissoluble community of interest as *one* nation. Any other tenure by which the West can hold this essential advantage, whether derived from its own separate strength, or from an apostate and unnatural connection with any foreign power, must be intrinsically precarious.

While, then, every part of our country thus feels an immediate and particular interest in union, all the parts combined cannot fail to find, in the united mass of means and efforts, greater strength, greater resource, proportionably greater security from external danger, a less frequent interruption of their peace by foreign nations; and, what is of inestimable value, they must derive from union an exemption from those broils and wars between themselves, which so frequently afflict neighboring countries, not tied together by the same governments; which their own rivalships alone would be sufficient to produce, but which opposite foreign alliances, attachments, and intrigues, would stimulate and embitter. Hence, likewise, they will avoid the necessity of those overgrown military establishments, which, under any form of government, are inauspicious to liberty, and which are to be regarded as particularly hostile to republican liberty; in this sense it is, that your union ought to be considered as a main prop of your liberty, and that the love of the one ought to endear to you the preservation of the other.

These considerations speak a persuasive language to every reflecting and virtuous mind, and exhibit the continuance of the Union as a primary object of patriotic desire. Is there a doubt whether a common Government can embrace so large a sphere? Let experience solve it. To listen to mere speculation, in such a case, were criminal. We are authorized to hope, that a proper organization of the whole, with the auxiliary agency of governments for the respective subdivisions, will afford a happy issue to the experiment. It is well worth a fair and full experiment. With such powerful and obvious motives to Union, affecting all parts of our country, while experience shall not have demonstrated its impracticability, there will always be reason to distrust the patriotism of those, who, in any quarter, may endeavor to weaken its bands.

In contemplating the causes which may disturb our Union, it occurs, as matter of serious concern, that any ground should have been furnished for characterizing parties by geographical discriminations—Northern and Southern—Atlantic and Western: whence designing men may endeavor to excite a belief that there is a real difference of local interests and views. One of the expedients of party to acquire influence within particular districts, is to misrepresent the opinions and aims of other districts. You cannot shield yourselves too much against the jealousies and heart-burnings which spring from these misrepresentations; they tend to render alien to each other those who ought to be bound together by fraternal affection. The inhabitants of our western country have lately had a useful lesson on this head; they have seen in the negotiation by the executive, and in the unanimous ratification by the Senate, of the treaty with Spain, and 'in the universal satisfaction at that event throughout the United States, a decisive proof how unfounded were the suspicions propagated among them of a policy in the general government, and in the Atlantic states, unfriendly to their interests in regard to the Mississippi:

they have been witnesses to the formation of two treaties—that with Great Britain and that with Spain, which secure to them everything they could desire in respect to our foreign relations, towards confirming their prosperity. Will it not be their wisdom to rely, for the preservation of these advantages, on the Union by which they were procured? Will they not henceforth be deaf to those advisers, if such there are, who would sever them from their brethren and connect them with aliens?

To the efficacy and permanency of your Union, a government for the whole is indispensable. No alliances, however strict, between the parties, can be an adequate substitute; they must inevitably experience the infractions and interruptions which all alliances, in all times, have experienced. Sensible of this momentous truth, you have improved upon your first essay by the adoption of a Constitution of government better calculated than your former for an intimate Union, and for the efficacious management of your common concerns. This government, the offspring of our own choice, uninfluenced and unawed, adopted upon full investigation and mature deliberation, completely free in its principles, in the distribution of its powers, uniting security with energy, and containing within itself a provision for its own amendment, has a just claim to your confidence and your support. Respect for its authority, compliance with its laws, acquiescence in its measures, are duties enjoined by the fundamental maxims of true liberty. The basis of our political systems is the right of the people to make and to alter their constitutions of government: but the Constitution which at any time exists, till changed by an explicit and authentic act of the whole people, is sacredly obligatory upon all. The very idea of the power, and the right of the people to establish government, presupposes the duty of every individual to obey the established government.

All obstructions to the execution of the laws, all combinations and associations, under whatever plausible character, with the real design to direct, control, counteract, or awe the regular deliberation and action of the constituted authorities, are destructive of this fundamental principle, and of fatal tendency. They serve to organize faction, to give it an artificial and extraordinary force; to put in the place of the delegated will of the nation the will of a party, often a small but artful and enterprising minority of the community; and, according to the alternate triumphs of different parties, to make the public administration the mirror of the ill-concerted and incongruous projects of faction, rather than the organ of consistent and wholesome plans, digested by common counsels and modified by mutual interests.

However combinations or associations of the above description may now and then answer popular ends, they are likely, in the course of time and things, to become potent engines by which cunning, ambitious, and unprincipled men will be enabled to subvert the power of the people, and to usurp for themselves the reins of government; destroying, afterwards, the very engines which had lifted them to unjust dominion.

Towards the preservation of your government, and the permanency of your present happy state, it is requisite not only that you steadily discountenance irregular oppositions to its acknowledged authority, but also that you resist with care the spirit of innovation upon its principles, however specious the pretext. One method of assault may be to effect, in the forms of the Constitution, alterations which will impair the energy of the system, and thus to undermine what cannot be directly overthrown. In all the changes to which you may be invited, remember that time and habit are at least as necessary to fix the true character of governments as of other human institutions; that experience is the surest standard by which to test the real tendency of the existing constitution of a country; that facility in changes, upon the credit of mere hypothesis and opinion, exposes to perpetual change from the endless variety of hypothesis and opinion; and remember, especially, that for the efficient management of your common interests, in a country so extensive as yours, a government of as much vigor as is consistent with the perfect security of liberty, is indispensable. Liberty itself will find in such a government, with powers properly distributed and adjusted, its surest guardian. It is, indeed, little else than a name where the government is too feeble to withstand the enterprises of faction, to confine each member of the society within the limits prescribed by the laws, and to maintain all in the secure and tranquil enjoyment of the rights of person and property.

I have already intimated to you the danger of parties in the state, with particular reference to the founding of them on geographical discriminations. Let me now take a more comprehensive view, and warn you, in the most solemn manner, against the baneful effect of the spirit of party generally.

This spirit, unfortunately, is inseparable from our nature, having its root in the strongest passions of the human mind. It exists under different shapes in all governments, more or less stifled, controlled, or repressed; but in those of the popular form it is seen in its greatest rankness, and is truly their worst enemy.

The alternate domination of one faction over another, sharpened by the spirit of revenge natural to party dissension, which, in different ages and countries, has perpetrated the most horrid enormities, is itself a frightful despotism. But this leads, at length, to a more formal and permanent despotism. The disorders and miseries which result, gradually incline the minds of men to seek security and repose in the absolute power of an individual; and, sooner or later, the chief of some prevailing faction, more able or more fortunate than his competitors, turns this disposition to the purposes of his own elevation on the ruins of public liberty.

Without looking forward to an extremity of this kind (which nevertheless ought not to be entirely out of sight), the common and continual mischiefs of the spirit of party are sufficient to make it the interest and duty of a wise people to discourage and restrain it.

It serves always to distract the public councils, and enfeeble the public administration. It agitates the community with ill-founded jealousies and false alarms; kindles the animosity of one part against another; foments, occasionally, riot and insurrection. It opens the door to foreign influence and corruption, which find a facilitated access to the government itself through the channels of party passions. Thus the policy and the will of one country are subjected to the policy and will of another.

There is an opinion that parties, in free countries, are useful checks upon the administration of the government, and serve to keep alive the spirit of liberty. This, within certain limits, is probably true; and in governments of a monarchical cast, patriotism may look with indulgence, if not with favor, upon the spirit of party. But in those of the popular character, in governments purely elective, it is a spirit not to be encouraged. From their natural tendency it is certain there will always be enough of that spirit for every salutary purpose. And there being constant danger of excess, the effort ought to be, by force of public opinion, to mitigate and assuage it. A fire not to be quenched, it demands a uniform vigilance to prevent its bursting into a flame, lest, instead of warming, it should consume.

It is important, likewise, that the habits of thinking in a free country should inspire caution in those intrusted with its administration, to confine themselves within their respective constitutional spheres, avoiding, in the exercise of the powers of one department, to encroach upon another. The spirit of encroachment tends to consolidate the powers of all the departments in one, and thus to create, whatever the form of government, a real despotism. A just estimate of that love of power, and proneness to abuse it, which predominates in the human heart, is sufficient to satisfy us of the truth of this position. The necessity of reciprocal checks in the exercise of political power by dividing and distributing it into different depositories, and constituting each the guardian of the public weal against invasions by the others, has been evinced by experiments, ancient and modern; some of them in our own country, and under our own eyes. To preserve them must be as necessary as to institute them. If, in the opinion of the people, the distribution or modification of the constitutional powers be, in any particular, wrong, let it be corrected by an amendment in the way which the Constitution designates. But let there be no change by usurpation; for though this, in one instance, may be the instrument of good, it is the customary weapon by which free governments are destroyed. The precedent must always greatly overbalance, in permanent evil, any partial or transient benefit which the use can at any time yield.

Of all the dispositions and habits which lead to political prosperity, religion and morality are indispensable supports. In vain would that man claim the tribute of patriotism who should labor to subvert these great pillars of human happiness, these firmest props of the duties of men and citizens. The mere politician, equally with the pious man, ought to respect and to cherish them. A volume could not trace all their connections with private and public felicity. Let it simply be asked, where is the security for property, for reputation, for life, if the sense of religious obligation *desert* the oaths which are the instruments of investigation in courts of justice? And let us with caution indulge the supposition, that morality can be maintained without religion. Whatever may be conceded to the influence of refined education on minds of peculiar structure, reason and experience both forbid us to expect that national morality can prevail in exclusion of religious principles.

It is substantially true, that virtue or morality is a necessary spring of popular government. The rule, indeed, extends, with more or less force, to every species of free government. Who, that is a sincere friend to it, can look with indifference upon attempts to shake the foundation of the fabric?

Promote, then, as an object of primary importance, institutions for the general diffusion of knowledge. In proportion as the structure of a government gives force to public opinion, it is essential that public opinion should be enlightened.

As a very important source of strength and security, cherish public credit. One method of preserving it is to use it as sparingly as possible; avoiding occasions of expense by cultivating peace, but remembering also that timely disbursements to prepare for danger, frequently prevent much greater disbursements to repel it; avoiding, likewise, the accumulation of debt not only by shunning occasions of expense but by vigorous exertions, in time of peace, to discharge the debts which unavoidable wars may have occasioned; not ungenerously throwing upon posterity the burden which we ourselves ought to bear. The execution of these maxims belongs to your representatives, but it is necessary that public opinion should co-operate. To facilitate to them the performance of their duty, it is essential that you should practically bear in mind that towards the payment of debts there must be revenue; that to have revenue there must be taxes; that no taxes can be devised which are not more or less inconvenient and unpleasant; that the intrinsic embarrassment inseparable from the selection of the proper objects (which is always a choice of difficulties) ought to be a decisive motive for a candid construction of the conduct of the government in making it, and for a spirit of acquiescence in the measures for obtaining revenue, which the public exigencies may at any time dictate.

Observe good faith and justice towards all nations; cultivate peace and harmony with all. Religion and morality enjoin this conduct; and can it be that good policy does not equally enjoin it? It will be worthy of a free, enlightened, and, at no distant period, a great nation, to give to mankind the magnanimous and too novel example of a people always guided by an exalted justice and benevolence. Who can doubt that, in the course of time and things, the fruits of such a plan would richly repay any temporary advantages which might be lost by a steady adherence to it? Can it be that Providence has not connected the permanent felicity of a nation with its virtue? The experiment at least is recommended by every sentiment which ennobles human nature. Alas! is it rendered impossible by its vices?

In the execution of such a plan nothing is more essential than that permanent inveterate antipathies against particular nations, and passionate attachments for others, should be excluded; and that, in place of them, just and amicable feelings towards all should be cultivated. The nation which indulges towards another an habitual hatred, or an habitual fondness, is, in some degree, a slave. It is a slave to its animosity or to its affection; either of which is sufficient to lead it astray from its duty and its interest. Antipathy in one nation against another disposes each more readily to offer insult and injury, to lay hold of slight causes of umbrage, and to be haughty and intractable when accidental or trifling occasions of dispute occur. Hence frequent collisions, obstinate, envenomed, and bloody contests. The nation, prompted by ill-will and resentment, sometimes impels to war the government, contrary to the best calculations of policy. The government sometimes participates in the national propensity, and adopts, through passion, what reason would reject; at other times it makes the animosity of the nation subservient to projects of hostility, instigated by pride, ambition, and other sinister and pernicious motives. The peace often, sometimes perhaps the liberty, of nations has been the victim.

So likewise a passionate attachment of one nation to another produces a variety of evils. Sympathy for the favorite nation, facilitating the illusion of an imaginary common interest, in cases where no real common interest exists, and infusing into one the enmities of the other, betrays the former into a participation in the quarrels and wars of the latter, without adequate inducement or justification. It leads also to concessions to the favorite nation of privileges denied to others, which is apt doubly to injure the nations making the concessions; by unnecessarily parting with what ought to have been retained, and by exciting jealousy, ill-will, and a disposition to retaliate in the parties from whom equal privileges are withheld; and it gives to ambitious, corrupted, or deluded citizens (who devote themselves to the favorite nation) facility to betray, or sacrifice the interest of their own country without odium; sometimes even with popularity; gilding with the appearance of a virtuous sense of obligation a commendable deference for public opinion, or a laudable zeal for public good, the base or foolish compliances of ambition, corruption, or infatuation.

As avenues to foreign influence in innumerable ways,

such attachments are particularly alarming to the truly enlightened and independent patriot. How many opportunities do they afford to tamper with domestic factions, to practise the art of seduction, to mislead public opinion, to influence or awe the public councils! Such an attachment of a small or weak towards a great and powerful nation dooms the former to be the satellite of the latter.

Against the insidious wiles of foreign influence (I conjure you to believe me, fellow-citizens), the jealousy of a free people ought to be *constantly* awake; since history and experience prove that foreign influence is one of the most baneful foes of republican government. But that jealousy, to be useful, must be impartial; else it becomes the instrument of the very influence to be avoided, instead of a defence against it. Excessive partiality for one foreign nation, and excessive dislike for another, cause those whom they actuate to see danger only on one side, and serve to veil, and even second the arts of influence on the other. Real patriots, who may resist the intrigues of the favorite, are liable to become suspected and odious; while its tools and dupes usurp the applause and confidence of the people to surrender their interests.

The great rule of conduct for us, in regard to foreign nations, is, in extending our commercial relations, to have with them as little political connection as possible. So far as we have already formed engagements, let them be fulfilled with perfect good faith. Here let us stop.

Europe has a set of primary interests, which to us have none, or a very remote relation. Hence she must be engaged in frequent controversies, the causes of which are essentially foreign to our concerns. Hence, therefore, it must be unwise in us to implicate ourselves, by artificial ties, in the ordinary vicissitudes of her politics, or the ordinary combinations and collisions of her friendships or enmities.

Our detached and distant situation invites and enables us to pursue a different course. If we remain one people, under an efficient government, the period is not far off when we may defy material injury from external annoyance; when we may take such an attitude as will cause the neutrality we may at any time resolve upon, to be scrupulously respected; when belligerent nations, under the impossibility of making acquisitions upon us, will not lightly hazard the giving us provocation; when we may choose peace or war, as our interest, guided by justice, shall counsel.

Why forego the advantages of so peculiar a situation? Why quit our own to stand upon foreign ground? Why, by interweaving our destiny with that of any part of Europe, entangle our peace and prosperity in the toils of European ambition, rivalship, interest, humor, or caprice?

It is our true policy to steer clear of permanent alliances with any portion of the foreign world; so far, I mean, as we are now at liberty to do it; for let me not be misunderstood as capable of patronizing infidelity to existing engagements. I hold the maxim no less applicable to public than to private affairs, that honesty is always the best policy. I repeat it, therefore, let those engagements be observed in their genuine sense. But, in my opinion, it is unnecessary and would be unwise to extend them.

Taking care always to keep ourselves, by suitable establishments, on a respectable defensive posture, we may safely trust to temporary alliances for extraordinary emergencies.

Harmony, and a liberal intercourse with all nations, are recommended by policy, humanity, and interest. But even our commercial policy should hold an equal and impartial hand; neither seeking nor granting exclusive favors or preferences; consulting the natural course of things; diffusing and diversifying, by gentle means, the streams of commerce, but forcing nothing; establishing with powers so disposed, in order to give trade a stable course, to define the rights of our merchants, and to enable the government to support them, conventional rules of intercourse, the best that present circumstances and mutual opinions will permit, but temporary and liable to be, from time to time, abandoned or varied, as experience and circumstances shall dictate; constantly keeping in view that it is folly in one nation to look for disinterested favors from another; that it must pay, with a portion of its independence, for whatever it may accept under that character; that by such acceptance it may place itself in the condition of having given equivalents for nominal favors, and yet of being reproached with ingratitude for not giving more. There can be no greater error than to expect or calculate upon real favors from nation to nation. It is an illusion which experience must cure, which a just pride ought to discard.

In offering to you, my countrymen, these counsels of an old and affectionate friend, I dare not hope they will make the strong and lasting impression I could wish; that they will control the usual current of the passions, or prevent our nation from running the course which has hitherto marked the destiny of nations; but if I may even flatter myself that they may be productive of some partial benefit, some occasional good; that they may now and then recur to moderate the fury of party spirit, to warn against the mischief of foreign intrigues, to guard against the impostures of pretended patriotism; this hope will be a full recompense for the solicitude for your welfare by which they have been dictated.

How far, in the discharge of my official duties, I have been guided by the principles which have been delineated, the public records and other evidences of my conduct must witness to you and the world. To myself the assurance of my own conscience is, that I have at least believed myself to be guided by them.

In relation to the still subsisting war in Europe, my proclamation of the 22d of April, 1793, is the index to my plan. Sanctioned by your approving voice, and by that of your Representatives in both Houses of Congress, the spirit of that measure has continually governed me, uninfluenced by any attempts to deter or divert me from it.

After deliberate examination, with the aid of the best lights I could obtain, I was well satisfied that our country, under all the circumstances of the case, had a right to take, and was bound in duty and interest to take, a neutral position. Having taken it, I determined, as far as should depend upon me, to maintain it with moderation, perseverance, and firmness.

The considerations which respect the right to hold this conduct it is not necessary on this occasion to detail. I will only observe, that, according to my understanding of the matter, that right, so far from being denied by any of the belligerent powers, has been virtually admitted by all.

The duty of holding a neutral conduct may be inferred, without anything more, from the obligation which justice and humanity impose on every nation, in cases in which it is free to act, to maintain inviolate the relations of peace and amity towards other nations.

The inducements of interest for observing that conduct will best be referred to your own reflections and experience. With me a predominant motive has been to endeavor to gain time to our country to settle and mature its yet recent institutions, and to progress, without interruption, to that degree of strength and consistency which is necessary to give it, humanly speaking, the command of its own fortunes.

Though, in reviewing the incidents of my administration, I am unconscious of intentional error, I am nevertheless too sensible of my defects not to think it probable that I may have committed many errors. Whatever they may be, I fervently beseech the Almighty to avert or mitigate the evils to which they may tend. I shall also carry with me the hope that my country will never cease to view them with indulgence; and that, after forty-five years of my life dedicated to its service with an upright zeal, the faults of incompetent abilities will be consigned to oblivion, as myself must soon be to the mansions of rest.

Relying on its kindness in this, as in other things, and actuated by that fervent love towards it which is so natural to a man who views in it the native soil of himself and his progenitors for several generations, I anticipate, with pleasing expectation, that retreat in which I promise myself to realize, without alloy, the sweet enjoyment of partaking, in the midst of my fellow-citizens, the benign influence of good laws under a free government—the ever favorite object of my heart—and the happy reward, as I trust, of our mutual cares, labors, and dangers.

George Washington.

United States, 17th September, 1796.

INDEX.

(The Numbers refer to the Pages of the work.)

THE END.

www.ingramcontent.com/pod-product-compliance
Lightning Source LLC
LaVergne TN
LVHW010215110826
845151LV00004B/1093

* 9 7 8 1 4 2 5 5 2 7 7 1 6 *